YOU
may be a
LIBERAL
if.....

Bob Sagan

A Self-Help Guide For Those Suffering
Identity Crises During These Times Of
Rampaging Liberal Irrelevance

authorHOUSE™

1663 LIBERTY DRIVE, SUITE 200
BLOOMINGTON, INDIANA 47403
(800) 839-8640
WWW.AUTHORHOUSE.COM

First published by AuthorHouse 01/12/2006

ISBN: 1-4208-9106-5 (sc)

Printed in the United States of America
Bloomington, Indiana

This book is printed on acid-free paper.

Dedication

For Dorothy and Mary, two great sisters, who always took the little kid to the beach

-and-

For Nancy, my beautiful wife, who continues to take the big kid to the cleaners

Contents

Introduction

"A liberal is a man too broadminded to take his own side in a quarrel"

-- Robert Frost

With both thanks and apologies to Jeff Foxworthy, this book's admittedly ambitious purpose is to attempt a clear defining of just what a "liberal" is. As unsavory as American politics have become (conservatives are allowed here to substitute *petty* and *personal, mendacious* and *mean-spirited*), they're too critical a part of our lives to be actively pursued by anyone going through an identity crisis.

Even that eminently objective, political pundit Michael Savage, Ph.D., has insisted that liberalism is a mental disorder – from his book titled (appropriately enough) *Liberalism is a Mental Disorder* (Nelson Current, Nashville, Tenn., 2005)

That keen observation was underscored, and the need for a scholarly tome such as this became apparent only recently, as increasing numbers of our left-leaning American cousins, formerly known as "liberals," began calling themselves *progressives*.

What is a *progressive*? I'm glad you asked. I was, at best, vague myself. An intriguing definition can be found at http://vikingphoenix.com, which warns that its service is "not for children or sissies" – *I accessed it anyway.* According to that website, "progressive" is defined as:

> "Statist using Marxist (leftist) methods and pretexts to progressively increase the power of the state; e.g., class warfare involving race, gender, sexual affinity, ecology and progressive taxation; as in multiculturalism, feminism and gay rights, environmentalism and confiscatory taxation, and rights to self defense, and frequently characterized by politically correct language. The lumpenproletariat are the shock troops used by progressives to increase the power of the state. A current method used by progressives to increase and hold political power is to create fresh lumpenproletariat by manipulation of immigration laws."

Got that?

I'm not sure, but it reads suspiciously like a *liberal* to me. In the advertising biz we used to employ a phrase – "perfuming the pig." Essentially, it meant taking the same old idea or concept and dressing it up – disguising it – for recycling. Same old pig…it just smelled different, but not necessarily better. So it beats me why anyone would prefer "progressive" to "liberal." Then again, what's in a name? *That which we call a pig by any other word would smell as sweet.* I told you this was a scholarly tome.

Actually, for those whose history is a little cloudy, a "Progressive Party" did exist back in the mid-forties, spearheaded by Henry Wallace, who served as Franklin Delano Roosevelt's vice president. When Roosevelt dumped Wallace in 1944 in favor of Harry Truman as his running mate, Wallace went on to found the Progressive Party, which as it turned out was Soviet-backed and Communist-riddled. Wallace ran on the Progressive ticket in 1948, pulled down about a million votes, and afterward was allowed to slip into obscurity. He should have been shot.

The idea in these pages is *not to argue* the case for what or whom a liberal is. Rather, it's to present for the reader this collection of some 300-odd items (some extremely odd) of unabashed liberal behavior, and let him *or her* make the call (as I take an unaccustomed stab at being *politically correct* in my syntax).

Reading these items, one after another, you may undergo an epiphany of sorts. So many incidents of liberal lies and lunacy have been only too well documented over the years. But to see them here, laid bare – one unbelievably ridiculous example after another – has a synergistic effect that can be at first infuriating, and then...*numbing*. For that reason, it's probably best to read only a few of these *mauvais mots* at one sitting, and then chill out and chew on those in order to appreciate the full effect. More on that later.

To be fair, the synergism mentioned is caused in part by the contextual isolation of some of these vicious vignettes – added to the sheer weight imposed by their numbers. Nevertheless, anyone who considers himself *something other than a liberal* and reads the following chapters can't help but ask – *Do we really share a commonality with these people who – like us – call themselves "Americans?"* How can anyone display this thinly disguised disdain for their homeland and such a cavalier concern for its well-being, and still claim even passable patriotism for the place? Here is where liberals conveniently would accuse the writer of "McCarthyism."

What I wrestle with mightily is this: Are liberals really as naïve as they represent themselves, or are they being disingenuous? I hope it's the *naïve thing;* otherwise they'd be nothing more than "Big Fat Idiots" – to paraphrase Al Franken (Hey, if you can't steal prolix from the great ones, don't steal at all).

It's easier to forgive a dumbass than a deceiver.

Personally, I think that being a little idealistic – aspiring to a world *that could be, should be* – is a good thing as long as we season that soufflé with a soupçon of common sense. There's nothing wrong with extending our reach for the stars, but we should keep one foot grounded in the real world while we're doing it. Otherwise, that's how we fall off barstools.

No one can hope to attain the ideal by ignoring the real – a little wordy for a bumper sticker, though it resonates.

But too many gomers are stomping around cloddishly in their self-generated ether, seemingly oblivious to the real world; indignantly taking the moral highground against anyone with the gall to suggest, for example, that people and families, and homes and jobs are more important than, say, *mythological animals*?

Smacking of the liberal persuasion, a group of federal and Washington State wildlife biologists were caught not long ago illegally trying to forbid public access to two national parks. They faked evidence that the parks were populated by a threatened wildcat species – the Canada lynx. The motivations may have been noble, but the machinations sucked.

One of the best ways to define a liberal, with reasonable accuracy, is simply by spotlighting some well-known paragons: Teddy Kennedy and Howard Dean are liberals – *big time*. In Hollywood, Woody Harrelson and Barbra Strident are streisand liberals (reverse that – or don't). Most any news media guy or gal is a liberal – about 80 percent. Everyone who ever was or ever will be members of PETA and the ACLU are liberals. A lot of unattractive people seem to be liberals. I'm glad you and I are not...liberals, I mean. I've had a lot of *first person* practice handling *unattractive*.

Granted, that *unattractive/liberal* pairing may not be fair. Then again, who cares? Paraphrasing the immortal lyrics of songbird Tina Turner, "What's *fair* got to do, got to do, got to do with it?" In my enthusiasm, I think I shoehorned an extra "got to do" in there.

This book differs from Jeff Foxworthy's *Redneck* registry in a number of ways, not the least of which is that Jeff's *vignettes* are falling-down funny – whether you relate to the country *zeitgeist* or not. At best, some of the offerings contained in these pages might be considered abidingly humorous; many are sadly pathetic; and a few border on the treasonous (good reasons to buy a book, every one). But, hopefully, they're pretty much on target and halfway enlightening.

As I put these items together, I noticed that they fell conveniently into 10 categories, e.g., *domestic affairs, media, the presidency, Congress, the Clintons,* etc. However, there was some overlapping to be expected. For example, where would you stick this one (*now that was uncalled for*)?

You may be a liberal... if you shared her pain with *New Yorker* film critic Pauline Kael, who could not believe Richard Nixon beat George McGovern for the presidency back in 1972. Though Nixon carried 49 states, Kael could only lament, "Nobody I know voted for Nixon."

Ed. Note: *Sadly, she was probably telling the truth.*

So, do we rightfully assign this item to the *media* chapter or to the one on *history*? Or maybe the *presidency*? Readers may disagree. Tough noogies, this is my book. Go do your own.

At the end of this screed I acknowledge many of today's finest conservative and/or just plain commonsense writers, reporters and all-around *good eggs*, who assisted – albeit unwittingly – as research sources and inspiration. Also, the Media Research Center was always there to reinforce the irrelevancies of liberal lollygagging, and the Fox News Channel ("We report, you decide") served as a wellspring of topical material. Writing down these issues proved much more cathartic than constantly screaming at the TV and then having to wipe the screen dry – another good motivator, while at the same time saving money on those costly Bounty paper towels.

Back to Jeff Foxworthy: In his *You Might Be A Redneck If This Is The Biggest Book You've Ever Read,* Jeff writes: "After 15 years, you'd think I would have heard every redneck joke conceivable. But hardly a day goes by that someone doesn't come up to me and say, 'Hey, Jeff, here's one I betcha haven't heard.' And many times they're right."

So if the reader does come across any pet *liberalisms* not touched on in these pages, have at it. I'd be thrilled to hear from you at Bobsagan@msn.com. I'll even credit you in the next book if I'm able to use the item. That and $3.50 will get you a cup of java at Starbucks.

By the way, I'll consider this modest effort an unqualified success if Al Franken comes out with a *rejoinder* book titled *You May Be a Big Fat Idiot Conservative Liar if....* Or something like that.

And a word of caution: Unless you are a liberal – *and you actually admit to it* – you probably will find it difficult to read too many of these vignettes in one sitting, as alluded to earlier. Side effects for *non-liberals* include frustration, nausea, rage, the heartbreak of psoriasis, palpitations, split-ends and discolored toenails. If the symptoms persist, position your head between your legs – below your heart – for about 60 seconds.

Should you be a *bona fide* liberal, and are similarly affected for some reason, the cure is the same; except while you're down there, buss your butt goodbye because you've got a long dry spell ahead of you, baby.

Finally, after all the denigration, there is a lot to be said for being a liberal…

Reno, Nevada
November 2005

Congress Incongruous

**"When a party and office holder differ as to how
the national interest is to be served, we must place
the first responsibility we owe not to our party
or even to our constituents, but to our individual
consciences."**

-- John F. Kennedy

Senate Minority Leader Harry Reid (D. Nev.),
speaking to Las Vegas high school students in May
2005 – with Americans troops still dying in the Middle
East – told the kids he believed President George Bush
was a "loser." Less than two months later, commenting
during the Karl Rove/CIA-leak hearings then going on
before the grand jury – and in an egregious display of
chutzpah before the TV cameras – Reid declared, "It's
time to quit playing partisan politics with our national
security."

The Associated Press (believe it or not) put together
a montage of "Harry Reid's Greatest Hits:" On CNN,
Reid called Federal Reserve Board Chairman Alan
Greenspan "one of the biggest political hacks we have
in Washington." In 2003, Reid spoke on the Senate
floor for 8-1/2 hours straight, upset that Republicans
planned to spend 30 consecutive hours talking
about four judgeships Democrats had blocked. He
characterized Republican Senate Majority Leader Bill

Frist as displaying "amateur leadership." He also was quoted as saying the president "was not being honest" in a previous conversation about Republican efforts to break Senate rules.

Let's see, to sum it all up: The President of the United States is a loser and a liar...the Majority Leader of the U.S. Senate is an amateur...and the Fed Chairman is a political hack. It seems Senator Reid is right – *it is time to quit playing partisan politics.*

One might surmise the Democrats in Congress are particularly upset with George Bush, because in winning two terms he's forced them to work hard for the first time in eight years – and for a full eight years at that – trying to ambush his every program while looking over their respective shoulders to make sure Republican challengers in their home states aren't gaining ground. How stressful! Although safer than most of his cohorts, even Teddy Kennedy appears to have lost some weight – or at least rearranged his corpulence.

Whereas, if either Al Gore or John Kerry had been successful in their presidential bids, the Dems in Congress could have gone back to business-as-usual, rubber-stamping every piece of socialist offal leaking out of the House that Bill Bilked.

To their credit, the outgunned Congressional Democrats have proved to be a formidable force at gumming up the works of government. It just goes to show that when they apply themselves, they're able to make an even greater mess of things than when they deal in good faith with a Democrat in the Oval Office.

Of course, their brothers and sisters on the other side of the aisle have scandalously abrogated their advantage and seem to forget that Republicans are supposed to be the majority party these days. At least that's what American voters decided. But whad'we know?

After all, most of us would probably reason that a piece of legislation should be declared a Senate Bill if it were voted affirmatively 59 to 41. So there you go.

...you were proud of a younger, though apparently priority-challenged Nancy Pelosi, who stood up in Congress to caution an America about to do battle with Iraq over the invasion of Kuwait in 1991, saying, "We take very seriously the environmental consequences of our actions."

Ed. Note: *Kill the enemy, boys, but don't trample the Scheherazade Prairie Dog's habitat while doing it.*

-ᴄ ❉ ⴾ-

...you chuckled when the U.S. Senate's top-ranking Democrat told school kids that their Republican president was a "loser," but you experienced high dudgeon a few weeks later when a presidential advisor opined that some liberals failed to act as red-blooded patriots after the 9/11 outrage.

-ᴄ ❉ ⴾ-

...it did not occur to you to ask Sen. Harry Reid (who made the aforementioned remark), *If George Bush is a "loser," what does that make Al Gore and John Kerry?*

Ed. Note: *Whoops! Almost forgot...Bush stole the first election.*

-ᴄ ❉ ⴾ-

...the irony escaped you that liberal elements in congress who rail against voluntary school prayer as unconstitutional, are equally vociferous when it comes to assuring that Guantanamo Bay terrorists have absolutely every religious guaranty, even though the prisoners' interpretation of Islam seems seriously skewed.

⊰ ✻ ⊱

...you probably preferred to ignore John Kerry's comment that, "I voted against the $87 billion in Washington yesterday [earmarked to finance the war and rebuild Iraq]...but let me make it clear, I'm for winning the war in Iraq."
Ed. Note: *May we see that trick again, Senator Houdini?*

⊰ ✻ ⊱

...it never occurred to you that *advice* and *consent*, as practiced by Congressional Democrats during George W. Bush's second term, is nothing more than a euphemism for *obstructionism*.

⊰ ✻ ⊱

...you never asked at what moment in American presidential history did *advice* and *consent* morph into *disagree* and *dictate*? And from the minority party no less.

⊰ ✻ ⊱

...in your mind Sen. Edward "Teddy" Kennedy demonstrates political relevance in 21st Century American politics.

※

...you hung on every word when Teddy Kennedy exposed the "fact" that the Iraq war had been planned long in advance of its prosecution. "This war was made up in Texas, announced in January to the Republican leadership that the war was going to take place, and was going to be good politically. The whole thing was a fraud," declared the Senator.

Ed. Note: *It actually may be reasonable to consider that last statement, coming as it does from the lifelong and still reigning liberal champion of duplicity. Who could better recognize the practice?*

※

..."Ready Teddy's" incisive remarks about the dangers posed by North Korea (uttered shortly before the Iraq war) made him sound like a cool, clear seeker of wisdom and truth. Except that, until that moment he had been 100% rock-solid behind our 1994 treaty with Pyongyang, which was "negotiated" by Bill Clinton with the inestimable help of Jimmy Carter...and cheated on repeatedly by the Koreans.

Ed. Note: *One can't help but wonder, at what exact point over an eight-year period did Kennedy do such an about face on North Korea, which suddenly had* *become "evil" just as George Bush called it – as in "axis of EVIL?"*

…you agreed with Sen. J. William Fulbright (D-Ark.), who in a 1982 congressional hearing said President Reagan was "playing a dangerous game" with the Soviets. "If it is a psychological game, it is a complex and delicate operation requiring experience and subtlety in its execution – qualities which are hardly the hallmark of this administration," Fulbright sniffed.

Ed. Note: *Must have been a case of beginner's luck for Reagan.*

...Sen. Dick Durbin (D. Ill.) and you agree that the terrorist prison facilities at Guantanamo Bay compare on the same level with Hitler's Nazi death camps and Stalin's gulags.

Ed. Note: *Durbin later apologized for his intemperate remarks...sort of. Democratic kingmaker Mayor Richard Daley of Chicago told him he was an idiot, which helped.*

...you overlooked remarks from otherwise articulate liberals such as New York Congressman Charles Rangel (D. Harlem), who said of Republicans, "They are all afraid to come out from under their hoods and attack us directly;" or erstwhile Democratic Senator Carol Mosely-Braun from Illinois, who cleverly nailed nationally syndicated columnist George Will: "George Will can just take his hood and go back to wherever he came from."

Ed. Note: *When they really want to vent on conservatives, liberals always seem to resort to calling them racists or Nazis. At the same time, the quality of that shrill diatribe is something more resembling a little girl who was just disappointed in losing the Queen of the May competition. Are Rangel and Mosely-Brown proud of the way Democrats take the African-American vote for granted?*

...it shocked you that U.S. troops stationed at the Guantanamo Bay detention center had the audacity to criticize Senators Kennedy and Durbin, as well as Sen. Daniel K. Akaka (D. Hawaii), when they visited the facility in 2005, for their past irresponsible remarks comparing Guantanamo to a Soviet gulag.

Ed. Note: *None of the three, usually outspoken anti-everything administration politicians, had any comments regarding the troops' admonishments.*

-¤ ❀ ¤-

...you were intellectualized by the always glib and incisive Sen. John Kerry, who first voted in favor of the Iraqi invasion right before he voted against it...or something like that.

-¤ ❀ ¤-

...the surprising number of Congressional Democrats who voted for the Iraq war resolution in October 2002, and then disavowed it immediately after the November elections, didn't strike you as strange.

Ed. Note: *One explanation might be they were all drunk in October and it took a month to sober up.*

-¤ ❀ ¤-

...it doesn't bother you that Democrats seemingly cannot support any major programs put forth by the Bush Administration – or worse, offer any positive alternatives of their own.

...you agreed with Sen. Pat Leahy (D–Vt.), who commented after the U.S. had invaded Grenada to rescue 1,000 Americans from Cuban and other Communist troops during Reagan's presidency: "We'd like to have another country to invade, but they can't find one small enough," said Leahy, noted for his witty repartee.

Ed. Note: *With all those Americans in harm's way, does it really matter the size of the country? Leahy later would be forced to resign from the Senate Intelligence Committee when it was revealed that he leaked classified documents to the media, compromising security.*

⊰ ✳ ⊱

...it didn't strike you as significant that the entire Supreme Court boycotted President Clinton's State of the Union address because of his blatant lies under oath, something unprecedented in our presidential history.

Ed. Note: *Even more significant, a few weeks later, every Senate Democrat voted to keep Clinton in office.*

⊰ ✳ ⊱

...you were outraged, with an eager assist from Bush-Bashers, that the president would leave Washington for a 33-day *vacation* during the "dog days" of August, even though a president always takes the White House with him in that that he's surrounded by everyone and everything he needs to continue the affairs of state.

Ed. Note: *The Bush-Bashers forgot to mention that Congress, at the same time, vacated the Foggy Bottom for 36 days; although it could mean something might finally get done in the Nation's Capitol. Some political wag has suggested only the D.C. bartenders will be aware of the Congressional absence in August.*

━✹━

…as an added motivator for a little outrage you need the following: Congress works 150 days out of the year's 365. Members make $150k per year, but "work" only five months ($30,000 per month). Part of that work includes fundraising while Congress is in session.

Ed. Note: *Next time you hear how underpaid Congressional members are remember that $150,000 extrapolated figures out to $360,000 per annum. Add to that a whole bunch of perks, and our elected representatives aren't doing badly for essentially attending meetings, going to exotic places on fact-finding tours, and posing for photo opps – not to mention the contacts made in case there's a life after Congress.*

━✹━

…you're in favor of the Senate's current voting practice, which means a bill is defeated even if 59 out of 100 senators vote for it, making the Senate not too unlike the UN Security Council, in which one country's veto can scuttle the will of the majority.

Ed. Note: *Whatever happened to "majority rule," the linchpin of Democracy? How ludicrous have we become? You can be sure liberals in the Senate will want to change the voting rule once Democrats get back into power.*

-=¤ ❋ ¤=-

...like some heavy-hitters in Congress, you believe it's perfectly reasonable that a timeframe be established and announced for pulling coalition troops out of Iraq.

Ed. Note: *It's sometimes difficult to understand how so many otherwise intelligent people seem to morph into complete and utter morons after punching in for work on Capitol Hill. So much the worse if this is disingenuousness passing for stupidity. If that's the case, it's despicable and should be known for what it is – "treason."*

-=¤ ❋ ¤=-

...you cheered Florida Democratic Sen. Bill Nelson, who came out in support of Cindy Sheehan, whose son was killed in Iraq. Nelson said Sheehan has "clearly become the symbol of all grieving mothers in this country."

Ed. Note: *After her meeting with the president in 2004, praising his caring and concern, Sheehan has become politicized to the point where she has labeled Bush the world's biggest terrorist...claimed the U.S. waged war on Iraq because of our Israeli interests...and that we've* *contaminated that country with radioactivity. No one every accused Sen. Nelson of understating anything.*

...liberal vice presidential candidate and trial lawyer John Edwards got your vote in 2004, though had his ticket won, lawyers would have gained control of all three branches of the government.

Ed. Note: *The last time that happened, in the 1990s, the U.S. established itself as the litigation capital of the world. Currently, lawyers make up 53 percent of the Senate, but only one-third of 1 percent of the U.S. population. Next time you hear Congressmen bemoaning their inadequate compensation, ask yourself why so many lawyers gravitate toward those poor paying jobs.*

History's Hypocrisies

After his surprise defeat at Saratoga – a pivotal battle that convinced the French to recognize the independence of the American colonies and turned the tide in their favor – British General "Gentleman" Johnny Burgoyne was asked by an aide how history would treat the battle. "History will do as history always has, sir. It will lie," Burgoyne replied.

Though there may not have been too many "liberal" colonists back then during our skirmish with the Brits (otherwise we'd all be playing cricket today instead of baseball), dubious historical accounts of those and other critical watersheds in our history have leached down to us over the generations and become solidly entrenched as part of the American experience. Many of them still are recounted in American schools today.

As long as we're here, let's stay with the American Revolution for a minute and check out a few other minor inconsistencies. It's as good as any other period for that.

Even today, most Americans believe someone named Betsy Ross sewed the first American flag together. Fact is, Betsy Ross did not come into prominence until around 1876, when some of her descendants thought it would make for a swell story to attract tourists as

Philadelphia readied for its centennial celebration. Most accounts say Francis Hopkinson, who also signed the Declaration of Independence, designed the first flag. There is no actual proof that Betsy Ross had anything to do with putting the flag together.

Paul ("one if by land, two if by sea") Revere was a silversmith and manufacturer of false teeth, who also volunteered to provide an early warning to the Concord Minutemen when the British were on their way. Revere and another patriot, Billy Dawes, set out on horseback when they saw the signal. Along the way, Samuel Prescott, a young colonist doctor joined them. Shortly after, Revere and Dawes were captured by the British and thrown into jail for a brief time. But Prescott managed to sneak through and warn the Minutemen, while Revere cooled his heels in the hoosegow. You might say it doesn't matter who warned whom, as long as the troops were alerted for the sake of the battle. Still, there goes another myth.

What don't we know about George Washington? On that cold and critical Christmas night in 1776, when he prepared to cross the Delaware, Washington got into the boat with one of his favorite generals – Henry "Ox" Knox, who tilted the scales at 280 pounds – a particularly huge human being for those days. As he climbed into the crowded vessel, Washington nudged Knox with the toe of his boot and said, "Shift that fat ass, Henry. But slowly, or you'll swamp the damn boat." Most of us never heard about this human side of the "Father of Our

Country." It's no big deal, but it is interesting. Weren't we told only that Washington uttered some prayerful words in the boat that night, consigning their fate to the deity?

The point in all this is that Gentleman Johnny Burgoyne was right: History does lie; or at the least, doesn't relate some of the better parts of the story – which is lying by omission. That's why in just the past few years a number of new popular history books (not school text books) have come out suggesting in their titles that history, as published until now, has been less than truthful. Check out *Lies My Teacher Told Me* by James W. Loewen, The New Press, New York; or *The Politically Incorrect Guide to American History* by Thomas E. Woods, Jr., Ph.D., Regnery Publishing, Washington, D.C.; or *Don't Know Much About History* by Kenneth C. Davis, Avon Books, New York.

What's so important about reporting history in faithful fashion?

Liberal media lied (and are still lying) about the infamous Vietnam Tet offensive of 1968, which was reported by the media as a military defeat for American troops, when in fact it was a victory. An immediate consequence of the bogus reportage was a 25 percent drop in public support for the war. Most Vietnam War experts agree the Tet offensive effectively marked the beginning of the end for American involvement in Viet Nam. And some may consider that a good thing...some not. Just remember, what eventually becomes *history* is first reported as *news* by the media.

Up to that point, no war in history had been more thoroughly covered in the media virtually as it occurred, and no war's outcome was more decidedly determined by its media coverage. But all that doesn't necessarily have anything to do with the truth.

That brings us to today, more or less, as we watch the liberal media already working their *mojo* on one of the biggest stories of the 20th century – the sudden and final chapter in the saga of the Soviet Union.

Anyone old enough to remember Ronald Reagan's presidency will recall the confidence with which he approached what he loved to call "the evil empire." Those words alone were enough to send some American liberals scurrying for their bomb shelters. Then later, when Reagan added the rest of the words: "*...whose last pages even now are being written,*" the remaining liberals joined their brethren, covering their heads and what manhood they still possessed as they ducked for safety.

By the time Reagan left office to be succeeded by his vice president George H. W. Bush, the die had been cast and there was no reversing the process. Within three years, the evil empire was evil no more. It ceased to exist, much to the delight of countless millions – especially in Eastern Europe. Would that it were greeted so joyfully in this country by American liberals.

It wasn't long after the USSR crumbled that the liberal media began rewriting history. The most generous members – believe it or not the *New York Times* was among them – gave Reagan a sniff and a nod for his efforts. Others claimed it was his predecessor presidents whose policies, such as they were, all contributed to the eventual denouement – which inexorably had been put in place more than 30 years earlier by Harry Truman and Dean Acheson. It goes on…and on, *ad nauseam*. And of course, the liberal media in retrospect contend that the Soviet Union wasn't all that strong to begin with; these being the same intrepid reporters who fitfully checked their racing pulses every time that *Wascally Weagan* honked the Big Red Bear's nose.

Anyway, that's what the liberal press has done and is trying to do to history, even as you read this. For a brief, yet highly entertaining and enlightening examination of the media handling of Reagan and the Cold War, see Chapter 8, "How Truman Won The Cold War During the Reagan Administration," from *Treason* by Ann Coulter, Crown Forum, 2003.

...you look back with pride on past Democratic presidential standard bearers, including George McGovern, Michael Dukakis and Walter Mondale – dynamic, resolute and bold leaders, every last one of them; and all with miserably failed campaigns.

Ed. Note: *The common sense of grassroots America continues to amaze...and please.*

❄

...it was easy for you to excuse an inexplicable breakdown in the journalistic standards of famed *New York Times* columnist Harrison Salisbury, who went to Vietnam in the mid-60s and reported that the U.S. was deliberately bombing civilian populations in the country. Only after the reports were published in the *Times* was it learned that Salisbury had borrowed "his facts" extensively from a North Vietnamese propaganda pamphlet.

Ed. Note: *A discordant note runs through much of this; that apparently any kind of half-truth or outright lie is justifiable if it accomplishes the "greater good," as defined by the perpetrator.*

❄

...you still refused to believe it when the government's top-secret Venona Report revealed in 1995, that many of those liberals accused of being spies – who were being ardently protected by other liberals during the Cold War – *actually were* agents in the employ of the Soviet

Union. With only about 2 percent of the intercepted Russian secret cables deciphered, nearly 350 red agents had been identified.

Ed. Note: *Turned out Sen. Joseph McCarthy was vindicated, though the New York Times and other liberal media hardly took note of it. To do so, would have stripped today's liberals of their favorite rallying cry anytime anyone questions their misplaced allegiances.*

⚜

...you ever knew, but chose to ignore, that the Truman Administration in 1948 almost indicted Whitaker Chambers, the former communist, who was responsible for outing Alger Hiss – whom many thought would someday be secretary of state – as a major spy in the employ of Moscow.

Ed. Note: *The administration, after having dragged its feet on the case for many months, decided it wouldn't be wise to try Chambers on perjury charges after public opinion shifted in his favor. Years later, President Reagan posthumously awarded Chambers America's highest civilian medal for his work.*

⚜

...you agreed with some in academia and government that Hiss may have been railroaded, so that when he was released from prison after 44 months, the government restored his pension, the Massachusetts bar reinstated him, and the *New York Times* published an op-ed piece written by him.

Ed. Note: *Amazingly, Hiss also was booked for speaking invitations at Columbia, Cornell, Harvard and Princeton. Bard College in New York has established an Alger Hiss Professor of Social Studies and NYU has created a website to help vindicate him. Yet, all the information that continued to come out in subsequent years, just further locked up the case against him.*

※

...the always-charismatic Andrew Young, Jimmy Carter's Ambassador to the United Nations, convinced you and other Americans to believe that "climate" was responsible for the poor harvests in the USSR, which resulted in the starvation deaths of millions of peasants. Only after the implosion of that system, did irrefutable evidence from the Russian archives reveal how generations of Soviet leaders used forced collectivization of agriculture to "cleanse" that society of undesirable elements.

Ed. Note: *Main targets of the "cleansing" were the "kulaks," nothing more than middle-income farmers, who were stripped of virtually everything they owned by the Soviet commissars. Only the most naïve (or disingenuous) of liberals could believe Russia had experienced several consecutive decades of bad crop weather as Andrew Young insisted.*

※

...you also accepted Andrew Young's *defense* of a harshly repressive Soviet society that "tried" some of its most distinguished citizens as traitors. After all, Young claimed, "hundreds, maybe thousands" of Americans in our jails at the time were political prisoners as well.

Ed. Note: *Even some liberals couldn't swallow that one. Eventually, Young was forced to resign his U.N. post because he violated the U.S. ban on meeting with terrorist groups, specifically the Palestinian Liberation Organization.*

⊰ ❋ ⊱

...you hearken back nostalgically to the Watergate break-in, as those good old days when the Democrats might still have had some ideas worth stealing.

Ed. Note: *Another bon mot from Jay Leno.*

⊰ ❋ ⊱

...if, like so many liberals, the thought never entered your mind that Communists never have won a free election anywhere, at anytime in the world. Yet liberals always insisted that such Soviet canards represented the popular will.

Ed. Note: *Some sage recently pointed out, after the implosion of the Soviet Union, that the USSR was the only country that held an empire together by virtue of its military alone, with absolutely nothing else to recommend it to its subjects – certainly not its economic policies.*

...you believe historical texts that venerate Franklin Delano Roosevelt for his New Deal programs, which purportedly provided jobs and economic stimulus, when in fact most leading economists today agree that said jobs were funded by taking money *from taxpayers* and giving it *to non-taxpayers*, resulting in no net stimulus.

-¤ ❈ ¤-

...you want to believe the history books that tell you FDR 's New Deal programs snatched America from the jaws of the Depression, in spite of the fact that unemployment from 1933 to 1940 (on his watch) averaged a horrific 18 percent.

Ed. Note: *Many biographers and economists believe Roosevelt was one of the more ignorant presidents in recent history when it came to creating wealth and economics in general.*

-¤ ❈ ¤-

...you can trace your proud political heritage back to the 1944 election when FDR decided to replace his vice president Henry Wallace with Harry S. Truman. Supposedly not known at the time was that Wallace was a communist, loyal to Moscow, who would have become president upon the death of Roosevelt a short time after the election.

Ed. Note: *Somehow "Give 'em hell, Henry" doesn't have quite the same pizzazz.*

...in the wake of the 2000 election being *stolen* from Al Gore (who still believes he won, at least secretly), you chose not to remember that Richard Nixon refused to contest the very close 1960 election results, even though solid evidence existed at the time that huge voter irregularities in Illinois (Mayor Richard J. Daley, Democrat) and Texas (Lyndon B. Johnson, Democrat) won the vote for John Kennedy.

Ed. Note: *Even President Eisenhower urged Nixon to contest the results, but Nixon refused, saying such an effort would seriously divide the American people. Years later, it was pretty well proved that family patriarch Joe Kennedy connived with Chicago mob boss Sam Giancana to win it for his son in Illinois, which pushed the Democrats over the top.*

⊰ ✳ ⊱

...you were around in the mid-70s, and would have cheered the University of California's affirmative action decision to twice reject Alan Bakke, a white, A-minus student, from attending the medical school *in favor of* a minority student (C+ grade average – in the bottom-third of applicants).

Ed. Note: *The student accepted in place of Bakke eventually became a doctor and was later suspended by the California medical board for his "inability to perform some of the most basic duties required of a physician." At least one death was associated with the case. Or...was it associated with affirmative action?*

...affirmative action run amok did not concern you when the U.S. Forest Service, in 1995, first posted a job announcement for firefighters that avowed, "Only unqualified applicants may apply." A later announcement refined that into, "Only applicants who do not meet [job requirement] standards will be considered."

Ed. Note: *The FDA's EEO Handbook also instructed that grammatical skills and accurate spelling requirements for secretarial and clerical positions should be de-emphasized because they made it tougher to attract "underrepresented" groups or individuals with disabilities.*

❦ ✳ ❧

...you chose to ignore Lenin's (Vladimir Ilyich not John) widely quoted prediction that "liberals and other weak-minded souls" in the West could be relied upon to be "useful idiots" as far as the Soviet Union was concerned.

Ed. Note: *It wasn't too many years after his prediction that events in the U.S. – occurring practically right up to the present day – would testify to Vladimir Ilyich's prescience, as American liberals practically tripped over each other excusing Soviet conduct, while at the same time excoriating U.S. foreign policy.*

❦ ✳ ❧

...you shook your head in disgust at unceasing media reports about the terrible economic times being visited upon the citizens of the former Soviet satellite countries, whom the media dutifully reported had seemed much better off under communism.

Ed. Note: *After 70 years of womb-to-tomb communism, no one even halfway smart expected a painless transition from one system to the next, save the liberal American media, apparently. Neither did the media revisit those countries later to showcase their impressive economic gains.*

-¤ ❀ ¤-

...after 50 years, you still invoke the term "McCarthyism" anytime someone suggests that certain American liberals display more than an abiding interest in making our adversaries look good at America's expense.

Ed. Note: *Commenting on the McCarthy-era hysteria, liberal journalist Nicholas von Hoffman wrote: "...point by point Joe McCarthy got it all wrong and yet was still closer to the truth than those who ridiculed him."*

-¤ ❀ ¤-

...you had trouble accepting that liberal *New York Times* reporter and Pulitzer Prize winner Walter Duranty, who reported glowingly on the USSR under Stalin, chose to ignore that Uncle Joe had killed at least 10-million Russians (mostly peasants) by starvation. Duranty won his Pulitzer for "dispassionate, interpretive reporting from Russia." But there was a far bigger story in what he didn't report, or distorted.

Ed. Note: *Only a few years ago it was learned that the Soviets had Duranty neatly secured by his "short and curlies," having discovered the reporter's somewhat unorthodox sexual proclivities, which would have been career-ending in those days.*

❈

...you'd have a hard time believing that President Truman rebuffed Winston Churchill when he made his famous "Iron Curtain" speech in Missouri in 1946. In fact, Harry apologized to Joseph Stalin and offered him the *U.S.S. Missouri* to taxi "Uncle Joe" back and forth across the pond so he could rebut Churchill here in the U.S.

Ed. Note: *Stalin, who portrayed himself to the Russian people as a war hero, was scared to death of flying. But he didn't use the Missouri either, preferring to let bygones be bygones. What a guy!*

❈

... it didn't strike you funny when Sen. Charles Percy, a Republican liberal from Illinois, complained that President Reagan had not yet held a summit meeting with a Soviet leader, only to have Regan reply, "I couldn't help it...they kept dying on me."

Ed. Note: *Soviet Premiers Andropov and Chernenko both passed on Reagan's watch shortly after taking office. American liberals are notorious for possessing* *a sense of humor so subtle that it's often impossible to observe.*

⚜

...during another display of Reagan humor, you became almost hysterical when the President quipped (unaware that a radio microphone was open), " My fellow Americans, I'm pleased to announce that I have signed legislation that would outlaw Russia forever. We begin bombing in five minutes."

Ed. Note: *Cut to: The Kremlin, where they understood Reagan was joking and took the remarks less seriously (obviously) than did American liberals.*

⚜

...you (or your father) were thrilled by the words of George McGovern at the 1972 Democratic Convention, who would go on to be his party's nominee for president that year. In response to a South Carolina Democrat who asked McGovern if he was suggesting we should beg the North Vietnamese to "give back our boys," McGovern replied "...begging is better than bombing."

Ed. Note: *McGovern lost the presidential race that year to Richard Nixon 49 states to 1. During World War II, he was a bomber pilot.*

⚜

...a classic case of "double-speak" by novelist Mary McCarthy would have eluded you. Returning from a

North Vietnam visit during that war, McCarthy was asked how she could be so gushing over America's enemy when it didn't even have a free press. Of course, she blamed America for the North's "self-imposed rationing system in the realm of ideas."

Ed. Note: *After the war, it seems no one asked McCarthy, nor did she volunteer, why nothing had changed in North Vietnam, including a shackled press.*

❈

...you agreed with on-again, off-again TV talk show host Phil Donahue (never a poster child for the virtue of *humility*), who presumed to speak for millions of Americans when he told his Soviet audience: "Some Americans worry when the Soviet Union expands...the vast majority of people in the United States admire you."

Ed. Note: *Such bloviating deserves a bitch-slapping.*

❈

...if 19th century African-American abolitionist Frederick Douglass' words rang hollow when he said, "...do nothing with us. Your doing with us has already played the mischief with us...and if the Negro cannot stand on his own legs, let him fall also. All I ask is give him a chance to stand on his own legs."

Ed. Note: *Apparently the War on Poverty was not that chance, as it turned out.*

❈

...you continue to believe that the War on Poverty, which was introduced by Lyndon Johnson in 1965, was the savior of American society. According to the CDC's Division of Vital Statistics, in 1965, only about 8 percent of Americans were born out of wedlock. In 2002, that number had skyrocketed to nearly 35 percent. In the poor neighborhoods, formerly called "ghettos," that figure is closer to an astronomical 80 percent.

Ed. Note: *The blame is placed squarely at the feet of the War on Poverty, which rewarded unemployment, single parenting and illegitimacy; another trenchant example of fixing a problem by throwing money at it.*

✦

...like so many other gullibles, you really believed that the boringly predictable crop failures Soviet farmers endured year after year – since about 1917 in fact – really were due to bad weather.

Ed. Note: *It was an inexplicably long and harsh stretch of intemperate climate – affecting all USSR agriculture for about eight decades straight – which did not seem to let up, coincidentally, until the evil empire went out of business. Hmmm.*

✦

...you still revere the handsome and vibrant young president who was assassinated in 1963, but almost solely because of his martyrdom – certainly not for an otherwise lackluster Presidency.

Ed. Note: *The chimera that was Camelot turned out to be a perfect factotum for the Kennedy years, as historians began uncovering a largess of less than admirable skeletons in the JFK closet, including the more minor – that his two best-sellers were largely ghost-written for him. Interestingly, Kennedy was Bill Clinton's personal hero. In retrospect, it's amazing the two men seemed to share much in common.*

–¤ ❀ ¤–

...you marveled at the prescience of Connecticut Senator Christopher Dodd, who criticized Ronald Reagan's support for the Nicaraguan Contras in their struggle with the Cuban- and Soviet-backed Sandinistas, accusing the administration of standing against "the tide of history."

Ed. Note: *In less than seven years that "tide of history" would collapse in the "dust bin of history," just as Ronald Reagan promised it would.*

–¤ ❀ ¤–

...you found yourself strangely disappointed after the *New York Times*, the major TV networks, and practically every Democratic politician on the planet had predicted an impressive victory for Nicaragua Communist Sandinistas at the polls, when in fact they ended up thoroughly thumped by the Reagan-backed Contras.

Ed. Note: *American liberals neglected to take into account a fairly important element – the vote. The*

Nicaraguan people selected as president someone who wanted nothing to do with the Sandinistas or their backers.

...during the 1984 presidential campaign, Democratic candidate Walter Mondale's words of wisdom captivated you: "The fact is, that four years of Ronald Reagan has [sic] made this world more dangerous. Four more will take us closer to the brink."

Ed. Note: *Mondale's words were prophetic, as it turned out. "Four more" did take us to the brink, and three years after that, the Soviets fell into the precipice.*

...you nod knowingly when liberals insidiously suggest Republicans are all but trying to bring back slavery, being generally ignorant of the fact that the Republican Party was created to oppose slavery. It was history's Democrats who defended the practice in the 19th century.

Ed. Note: *Republicans were known as "The Whigs" at the time. As Casey Stengel used to say, "You can look it up."*

33

Homeland Chutzpah

"We live in fictitious times. We live in the time where we have fictitious election results that elect a fictitious president. We live in a time where we have a man who's sending us to war for fictitious reasons."
-- from Michael Moore's Oscar Acceptance Speech

The inequities of liberal machinations in the homeland – aided by the elitist media – often create a double standard (liberals v. *everyone else*) that no one should have to suffer.

In 1994, then Speaker of the House Newt Gingrich accepted a $4.5 million book advance from HarperCollins. Immediately, democrats and the liberal news media jumped on it, suggesting somehow it was improper, and that the Speaker should refuse the advance or donate it to "an orphanage." It was even suggested by CBS's Dan Rather that the advance might be a thinly disguised bribe (HarperCollins is owned by Australian media mogul Rupert Murdock, if that means anything). Other liberals didn't want Gingrich to publish the book at all – and that was *after* he already had announced he would turn down the advance.

Fast-forward to 2000 and Hillary Clinton, who had just accepted an $8 million advance for a *ghostwritten* tome on her White House years from Simon & Schuster (the highest bidder, big surprise!). The news media were conspicuous by their eerie silence – silence, at least, in that there was almost zero controversial commentary among the elitist press. Dan Rather apparently had lost his voice by that time. When Harry Reid (D. Nev.), who was then the vice chair for the Senate Ethics Committee, was appropriately asked about the advance, he opined that it was "wonderful."

Gingrich's *scandalous* publishing deal led to a ban on future book advances for House members. Clinton's apparently not so scandalous deal, though it was for almost twice the money, had no effect on Senate rules and generated no calumny from the liberal press. Maybe Gringich's mistake was in not holding out for more money. NAAAHHHH!

The reason it was permissible for Hillary, and not for Newt, according to a CNN reporter (Greta Van Susteren, before she went to Fox), was because an *authoress* was "finally able to go out into the marketplace and command a huge pile of money as an advance," and a lot of men [presumably non-liberals], were carping over it. The suggestion is, that because this particular author is from the *distaff* side, the ethics and standards of propriety applied to Gingrich are suspended in the case of Clinton.

That, ladies and gentlemen, is the quintessential *double standard.* It happens a lot in the homeland, and is often occasioned by one of the sorriest and most ludicrous cabals ever foisted on the American people (maybe even more fatuous than *feminism*); one that insidiously has seeped into just about every part of our lives, including our grammatical syntax. You may have heard of it – ***Political Correctness?***

As mentioned at the beginning of this chapter, the liberal media only compound the problem, especially if they can victimize a high-ranking Republican in the bargain. One more thing: Newt Gingrich returned his $4.5 million advance. Hillary Clinton held on to her $8 million.

...in the spring of 2005 you agreed that a *Newsweek* reporter should not be punished for refusing to reveal the source of his information that appeared in a story which *outed* CIA agent Valerie Plame, citing freedom of the press; but changed your mind that summer when it was revealed that the source of the leak appeared to be none other than Karl Rove, senior adviser to George Bush and architect of his campaign to defeat Democratic presidential candidates two campaigns running.

-❧ ❋ ❧-

...it was about time, as far as you were concerned, that smoking in California prisons became *verboten*. Except, of course, for those who employ the "sacred use" of tobacco in prayer and other religious ceremonies.
Ed. Note: *The politically correct prediction here is that not only will more Native American prisoners become born-again whatever, but also prison officials across the state suddenly will find they have incarcerated far more Indians than previously imagined.*

-❧ ❋ ❧-

...you thought it's about time the National Collegiate Athletic Association (NCAA) cracked down on schools using Native American names for their sports teams, as the NCAA ruled that no teams would be allowed to compete in any post-season championship games if they displayed such mascot names. Compounding the *politically correct* stupidity, the NCAA commissars ruled a North Carolina college could continue using its "Braves" name because 20 percent of the student body is Native American. But the Florida State University Seminoles would have to scrap its name – even though the Seminole tribe had expressly given FSU the green light to continue its usage.

Ed. Note: *Reduced to its ad absurdum, PETA should now be able to demand that teams also stop denigrating animals by using them as team mascots. Lions and Tigers and Bears, oh my!*

-◄ ❋ ►-

...your home on Beacon Hill and your summer place on The Cape are accessorized in every room with a fireplace mantle (fireplace optional), an Orvis tweed jacket (complete with elbow patches) and a Meerschaum, which allow you – at a moment's notice over chardonnay and sushi – to wax brilliant for your guests on the sad, sorry state of the downtrodden and disenfranchised in this country under a Republican administration.

-◄ ❋ ►-

...well intentioned, though ignorantly, you agreed that a Caucasian staffer with the mayor's office in Washington, D.C., should be terminated because he used the word "niggardly" in a meeting with other staff members – both African-Americans.

Ed. Note: *A poster-child example of PC run amok, "niggardly" goes back to the 14th century and means* "miserly." Particularly "upset" by the use of the "N word" was one of the staffers who, reportedly, wanted the "racist's" job.

-≒ ❋ ≓-

...you believe the government has the right to dictate to a small business owner whom he should be hiring, and in what numbers, to help ensure his company's success.

Ed. Note: *In a classic case, a small lamp manufacturer in Chicago was put on notice that he should be employing a certain percentage of non-white laborers. Checking his books, the owner discovered he actually employed more than the necessary "quota," and notified the government he would begin terminating some of his non-white employees in order to comply with its dictates (he was kidding, but of course the government doesn't "get" jokes).*

-≒ ❋ ≓-

...as far as your concerned, affirmative action is a fair and reasonable way to encourage cultural diversity in schools, and not some politically correct method of preventing many of the best and brightest young people their rightful admission to the colleges or universities of their choice.

-≒ ❋ ≓-

...you concurred with mothers in Houston who petitioned a Texas school board to fire those elementary school principals who did not speak Spanish, since their little darlings had not learned the language at home and thus were disadvantaged.

Ed. Note: *No one reported what percentage of the Spanish-speaking students involved were illegals. It was thought, however, that all the principals at risk were American citizens.*

❄

...the compassionate juices overflowed when you heard that San Francisco's board of supervisors voted in favor of funding sex change operations for S.F. City employees, costing taxpayers up to $50,000 for each "sex reassignment."

❄

...you prefer the euphemistic "entitlements" to that old standard, "welfare," when it comes to government largesse. Of course, you also favor "homeless" over "hobo/bum."

Ed. Note: *Editor is willing to concede that Lyndon Johnson's "Great Society" may have cured the societal ills that created hobos and bums – of course, it did so by renaming them "homeless."*

❄

...you're convinced that the American Civil Liberties Union is out there protecting the little guy, even after it continues to defend the North American Man Boy Love Association (NAMBLA), a national organization of pedophiles.

Ed. Note: *Not generally known is that the ACLU is subsidized by American taxpayers, enabling it to declare war on the Boy Scouts, the U.S. military, Christmas displays, and other American traditions. Check out United States Code 1988, which requires taxpayers to pay attorneys in civil rights cases. That includes You Know Who.*

◄ ✳ ►

...as far as you're concerned, American environmentalists are correct in "protecting" the 19 million-plus acres of The Arctic National Wildlife Refuge in northern Alaska from oil drilling, though by all accounts the estimated 10.3 billion barrels (twice that of Texas) could easily be recovered from roughly 1.5 million acres, or less than 10 percent of the total area.

Ed. Note: *Modern technology and science guarantee no harmful effect on flora or fauna. In fact, the construction of the Alaska pipeline nearly 30 years ago – trumpeted by doomsayers as an ecological Armageddon – actually improved caribou herd numbers, while supplying roughly 20 percent of our domestic oil. Just ask the local Inuit (Eskimo, to you).*

◄ ✳ ►

...PETA's (People for the Ethical Treatment of Animals) policies make sense to you, including the criminal release of 10,000 mink from a Washington farm a few years back. Not only did the mink become roadkill, but also those that survived decimated surrounding farm animals.

Ed. Note: *Some of the adjoining farmers suffered up to 50 percent loss among their chickens, ducks and geese. Even farm dogs were attacked.*

❈

...you probably concurred with the four Massachusetts Supreme Court justices who not long ago overthrew a 300-year-old law and ruled that the state's definition of marriage as a legal union between a man and a woman was "irrational".

Ed. Note: *Such rampant irrationalism in Massachusetts goes a long way toward explaining Teddy Kennedy's political longevity.*

❈

...you welcomed the recent parade of ACLU efforts and federal court decisions to interfere in church-state relations, even though the First Amendment clearly does not grant such powers to the feds.

❈

...you subscribe to the notion that racial minorities need government's helping hand to succeed, which of course suggests they are inferior to whites who apparently can make it on their own.

Ed. Note: *Those same people who advocate affirmative action, racial quotas and political correctness in other businesses wouldn't think of helping out a "poor white boy" trying to break into the NBA, which is disproportionately-populated with African Americans who make up only about 12 percent of our population. Unlike other businesses, it appears professional basketball teams have the luxury of hiring those "workers" whom they think will benefit their business best. Novel concept, that.*

⊷ ✦ ⊶

…the scenario replays itself with you as far as women in the job market are concerned, especially if you've bought into that shopworn argument that women earn only 75 cents for every dollar a man makes.

Ed. Note: *If as a business owner you could cut a significant part of your overhead by 25 percent simply by changing your hiring practices, would it make any sense to keep a lot of men on your payroll?*

⊷ ✦ ⊶

…you thought it a spirited prank that President Clinton's staff trashed the White House before George and Laura Bush moved in. Of course, those mainstream media that did deign to report the incident did so with a healthy skepticism over whether the vandalism occurred at all.

Ed. Note: *When Republicans chose to soft-pedal the incident for some reason, William Raspberry, Washington Post columnist, asked, "Can it be because the alleged vandalism never happened either?" About a year later, the General Administration Office issued the report that set the damage at $15,000.*

❋

...the $1.9 billion earmarked for combating HIV and AIDS in this country in 2004, fell short of expectations, because various self-interest groups had convinced liberal media (and therefore, you) that it wasn't enough.

Ed. Note: *By contrast, the Centers for Disease Control requested only $192-million (or 10% of that spent for HIV/AIDS) for treating various cancers in 2004. Yet, cancer killed more than 35 times the number of Americans in 2003 than did AIDS – which is, to a great degree, a preventable disease.*

❋

...the *federal* funding of San Francisco workshops – facilitating how gays can meet gays, have various kinds of sex, and still stay safe – was okay with you.

Ed. Note: *Workshops such as "Flirt, Date, Score" and "Bootylicious" offered advice on sex with male prostitutes, anal and oral intercourse. Your tax dollars at work.*

❋

...it's difficult for you to accept that in the U.S. there should be anybody who doesn't have health insurance, which means you probably agree with Hillary Clinton's universal health care plan, or something like it. The U.K. and Canada have it, and nobody seems too thrilled with it. Not the patients in Canada, not the doctors in Britain.

Ed. Note: *Many people don't realize that federal law in the U.S. requires hospital emergency rooms to treat anyone in need, regardless of whether they actually have insurance. That's one reason American patients who are insured end up paying more than they would otherwise – to pick up the slack caused by the uninsured.*

❈

...you thought justice done in 1994 when an activist U.S. District Court judge overturned Proposition 187 (which *denied* health care, welfare and education benefits to illegals), even though Californians had voted overwhelmingly *for* Prop. 187.

Ed. Note: *The ACLU was instrumental in 187's overthrow. Surprise!!! So much for the Will of the People.*

❈

...you ignored even the Red Cross being *politically correct* as it pleaded for more type-"O" blood donations, describing that type as the "most often requested," which in this case is really a euphemism for "most common."

Ed. Note: *See what happens when we indulge political correctness? The Red Cross feared it would offend type-"O" donors by pronouncing their blood "most common," thereby suggesting perhaps the donors themselves were "common."*

-ᅴ ❊ ᅡ-

...it seemed the punishment fit the crime when Orange Coast College in California suspended Kenneth Hearlson, a professor of political science, after he told his class that he wanted to see the Arab world stand up and condemn the events of 9/11.

Ed. Note: *On the other hand, History Professor Richard Berthold at the U. of New Mexico, told his class, "Anyone who can blow up the Pentagon has my vote." No retribution there, though the professor did apologize later.*

-ᅴ ❊ ᅡ-

...people such as the late Betty Friedan and the National Organization of Women (NOW) have defined your world as to how you view a woman's place in American society. And, according to NOW, it's not good.

Ed. Note: *American women possess more than half the wealth in this country and make up more than half our college students. The distaff side also is responsible for more than 50 percent of the applicants to law and* *medical schools. Women represent more than half the voters and outnumber men in all but two states. It's time men stayed home and took care of the house. Maybe we'd live longer.*

...you run right out and buy every new book by Doomsayer Paul Ehrlich (*The Population Bomb*), who has never been right in any of his major predictions over the past 40 years. Only TV weather forecasters come as close to being so wrong so often.

Ed. Note: *Despite Ehrlich's prognostications, Europe's population today is below replacement levels, the world sits on food surpluses, and the resurgent Ice Age scare has now morphed into one of global warming. Yet they keep throwing accolades – and money – at him. Where do I get a job like that?*

...the cockles of your heart are warmed by reports of American school kids contributing their dimes and quarters to protect endangered species in the U.S.

Ed. Note: *Of the roughly 400 "animals" listed as endangered, only about 65 are mammals. The rest are insects, fish, clams and snails, most of which none of us will see in our lifetimes anyway – and wouldn't recognize if we did.*

...everybody you know is certain that nuclear energy is a disaster just waiting to happen and points to the 1979 Three Mile Island nuclear plant incident as proof. As Dr. Morris E. Chafetz (an M.D.) points out in *Big Fat Liars* (Nashville, Tenn.: Nelson Current, 2005), more people will die from *rabies* in the U.S. this year than have died due to radiation in the entire history of the U.S. nuclear energy industry.

Ed. Note: *Nobody died, nobody was even injured at Three Mile Island. For another, more politically-oriented (and scathing) analogy regarding Sen. Edward Kennedy, check out "The Environmental Mess" (chapter six) of Chafetz's book.*

＊

...you're all for this conundrum, even though you can't explain it: Initially in favor of nuclear power's use to generate electricity, environmental movements abandoned the idea in the eighties, but not in favor of fossil fuels, which create significant pollutants. Alternative energy sources – hydroelectric, geothermal or wind – are cleaner, but the technology is either incipient, not available everywhere, or prohibitively expensive as it stands today.

Ed. Note: *It would seem many environmentalists would be happy only if we used no energy at all.*

＊

...your heart bleeds for many who commit crimes because of outside circumstances over which they have no control – often traceable to a horrid childhood. In short, you deny any linkage between criminal conduct and individual responsibility. As a result, more criminals spent more time out of the slammer, and guess how they occupied their free time?

Ed. Note: *The process began reversing itself in the 1990s, after U.S. communities – sick and tired of the situation – went back to prosecuting crime as they had previously, before the liberal hand-wringing got in the way of due process and common sense.*

⊰ ❋ ⊱

...the always lovely and talented Michael Moore acted as your *unofficial* spokesman at the 2003 Motion Picture Academy Awards as he accepted his Oscar, and then went into a semi-hysterical rant about George Bush being a "fictitious president;" and how, "We are against this war, Mr. Bush. Shame on you, Mr. Bush."

Ed. Note: *Resembling nothing so much as an unmade bed on stage, it is said Moore did irreparable damage to the tuxedo industry that evening while raising Bush's approval ratings by 5 points.*

⊰ ❋ ⊱

...the high cost of U.S. prisoner incarceration, roughly $30,000 per inmate, per year is your argument for lighter sentences and greater rehabilitation; while you ignore that the rate of criminal recidivism costs taxpayers about $200,000 per individual, per year while the criminal is on the outside.

-⊨ ❊ ⊨-

...whether an attorney yourself or not, you think the nation's lawyers are getting a bum rap about being blatantly opportunistic and avaricious. Apparently they don't agree with you in Virginia, where in 2002, complaints were filed against nearly 15 percent of the state's lawyers. That compares with dentists (6 percent); physicians/surgeons (4 percent); and nurses (0.5 percent).

Ed. Note: *What goes around comes around. In the U.S., the client-lawyer ratio is 290 to 1. In Great Britain it's 690 to 1; 2,450 to 1 in France; and in Japan, the ratio is 8,150 people to a single lawyer.*

-⊨ ❊ ⊨-

...you never recognized that anti-war activist Cindy Sheehan, who played the *squatter* near President Bush's Texas ranch, was "taken over" and exploited by leftist anti-war groups, who pumped money, personnel and support into her efforts to condemn the Iraq war. Sheehan emerged from her liberal makeover as a strident harpy, who would be satisfied only by a meeting with the President, though he had met with her the year before – and which was reported on very favorably by Sheehan herself.

Ed. Note: *The sudden change in Sheehan's demeanor and pronouncements suddenly came about in mid-August 2005, when her postings began appearing on leftist filmmaker Michael Moore's website, and she was clearly seen prior to TV interviews being prepped and "handled" by unidentified individuals presumed to be media consultants.*

International Irrational

**"And that's the world in a nutshell – an
appropriate receptacle."**

-- Stan Dunn

Perhaps only Ronald Reagan's presidency could approach that of George W. Bush's years in office for the sheer *rancor* and *revulsion* they've inspired among the left-leaning "loyal opposition" in America.

No doubt either man is/would have been proud to be associated with the other in that regard, since they both gave and are giving the liberals fits over their popularity with Americans. Both men have been considered simplistic in their approaches to matters of state. Both have been "apparently reviled" as *cowboys – apparently* because there are still plenty of us in the American West who don't think so badly of that term.

History still has plenty of cards to deal to Bush in the high-stakes poker game he's playing, and so far playing reasonably well, particularly in view of the hate-filled hypocrites he faces at home; while Ronald Reagan already has cashed in his chips (with all due respect) and come up a huge winner – even though liberal re-writers of history will have something to say about that as the years pass. At least you and I won't forget.

Still, the unassailable facts are that Reagan stuck it to the Soviets in no uncertain terms, confident that the "evil empire" (Democrats/liberals, here's where you're supposed to cringe) could not win a "guns and butter" competition with an America willing and able to display the resolve necessary to carry that competition to its agreeable conclusion.

Somehow Reagan knew. When even his most ardent supporters had some doubts about the Strategic Defense Initiative (and it was gleefully belittled and ballyhooed as "Star Wars" by his domestic adversaries), *Reagan knew...*

It's questionable whether Reagan himself really believed the SDI technology would prove feasible, but when Soviet Premier Mikhail Gorbachev first capitulated at the Reykjavik talks – and then folded the Soviet tent a few years later – the Star Wars technology actually became moot, didn't it? As long as Gorby believed it, just the *threat* of a successful SDI was by itself enough.

And maybe, that was what Reagan really knew. What a masterful job of bluffing that would have been, if it were so.

As a postscript to the Reagan legacy, former Soviet Foreign Minister Alexsandr Bessmertnykh told a post-Cold War meeting at Princeton University, "SDI made us realize we were in a very dangerous spot...Gorbachev was convinced any attempt to match Reagan's Strategic

Defense Initiative...would do irreparable harm to the Soviet economy."

There we have it right from the Russian bear's maw. In years to come, when liberal historians play fast and loose with history, as they most certainly will, you need only recall the above quote to put everything back into historical perspective.

And you only need to remember that first, the liberals said SDI never would succeed. After it did succeed (at least as a theoretical scare tactic), the naysayers claimed the Soviets never were all that strong to begin with. And they weren't. But nobody, most definitely not the naysayers, knew that.

...in the late 1980s, you did not share with President Reagan (and not even with the terrified Soviets), the faith in America's resolve and capability to topple the "Evil Empire."

Ed. Note: *After initially predicting that our "cowboy" president could be steering us on a course toward nuclear Armageddon, liberals changed gears and said the Soviets never were that strong to begin with – once the Soviet Union had imploded.*

...you really believed Mikhail Gorbachev willingly initiated, and was most instrumental in, the fall of the Berlin Wall and the dissolution of the Soviet Union – a feat for which *Time* named him "Man of the Decade."

...Reagan's "Berlin Wall" speech scared you as much as it did most of this country's media and just about everyone else calling himself a liberal. Even the "tea and cucumber sandwich" professionals in the State Department wanted to strike the passage in Reagan's speech telling Gorbachev to pull down the Berlin Wall.

Ed. Note: *But that was the part Reagan liked best, so it stayed in.*

...you agreed with the always-perspicacious Eleanor Clift from *Newsweek,* who explained why Ronald Reagan was so right, and the liberals so wrong about the USSR's imminent demise. Cliff contented, "People who want to give Ronald Reagan the entire credit for the collapse of the Soviet Union ignore the fact that the Soviet economy was collapsing [anyway] and the Reagan Administration covered it up."

Ed. Note: *Of course, this is the same reporter who, in commenting on Elian Gonzalez and whether the child should be returned to Cuba, said: "Frankly, to be a poor child in Cuba may, in many instances, be better than being a poor child in Miami." That must be why so many Cuban parents have been risking their lives to bring their poor children to the U.S.*

-¤ ※ ¤-

...it pleased you that John Kerry suggested the French tacitly were supporting him in his bid for the presidency against incumbent Bush in 2004, though why any American presidential candidate would even hint at French support is beyond comprehension.

Ed. Note: *Leave it to a liberal to glory in such a relationship with a country that has done everything within its power – third rate power though that may be – to try and thwart the U.S. and its policies at every turn. The U.S. can point to outright enemies from the not-too-distant past who have proved a truer friend by far than this "ally."*

…you've been tempted to throw in your lot with some of your more rabid leftist friends, who insist America's principal reason for involvement in the Middle East is *oil*, when in fact, it would have been easier, faster and cheaper for the U.S. to have grabbed Mexican or Venezuelan oil fields any time it wished.

Ed. Note: *Or, we could have commandeered the Kuwaiti or Iraqi oil supplies after the first Gulf War in 1991, when there was no one to oppose us, and since we already were in the neighborhood at the time.*

✦

…you agreed with Washington Democratic Congressman Jim McDermott, speaking from Baghdad, who claimed a U.S. President lied to the American people in order to pull their country into a war, strongly suggesting we should believe Saddam Hussein before we believe Bush.

Ed. Note: *Nationally syndicated columnist George Will said, "…I consider [McDermott's performance)] the most disgraceful performance abroad by an American official in my lifetime, something not exampled since Jane Fonda sat on the antiaircraft gun in Hanoi to be photographed…"*

✦

…you're quick to subscribe to the notion that we've dropped the ball in post-war Iraq, even though electricity generation exceeds the pre-war average…approximately

200 private newspapers are publishing...roughly 250 hospitals and 1,500 health clinics are operating...more than 30 million vaccinations have been given to Iraqi kids, and most of the court system is functioning.

Ed. Note: *Also, Saddam Hussein is being entertained in the slammer. And, at this writing, his two sons are still dead.*

⊰ ✸ ⊱

...as far as you're concerned, democracy has almost no chance of succeeding in the Middle East, though it's flourishing in Israel even under constant attack from without; and you ignore the establishment of successful democracies in countries with no previously democratic traditions, including Japan, Germany, India and several Latin American nations.

⊰ ✸ ⊱

...you honestly believe in the "New World Order," which promotes the one world concept that says we're all basically the same human beings, widely diverse cultural differences notwithstanding.

Ed. Note: *"Here, Mustafa, my beloved son, strap on this jacket, walk over to the crowd in that pizza parlor, and press this button."*

⊰ ✸ ⊱

...it's difficult for you to support Israeli *aggression* against the *peaceful overtures* of the Palestinians, especially since America's support of Israel has helped bring down the wrath of Islamic terrorism on our heads.

-≡ ❋ ≡-

...all those rosy economic pronouncements about the USSR by American liberal economists, including John Kenneth Galbraith (as late as the 1980s), caused you to wonder if the American capitalist system could compete with communism.

Ed. Note: *After its fall in 1991, westerners learned the USSR had the living standards of a Third World country. Even Moscow hospitals hardly could claim sewage, hot water, or running water. The hinterlands were worse. Why didn't experts like Galbraith know that? Why didn't our media? Why didn't Eleanor Clift? She knows everything else.*

-≡ ❋ ≡-

...Ronald Reagan's anti-Soviet rhetoric scared you, even though it was greeted with enthusiasm in Iron Curtain countries such as Poland, where Bartak Kaminski, a university professor, said Reagan was the first world leader who was willing to express ideas about the USSR that were shared by most Poles.

Ed. Note: *Even the first foreign minister of the Russian Republic said that the USSR was not a collection of republics, but rather "an evil empire, as it was once put..."*

...France's attitude toward the U.S. always has been understandable – as long as they weren't in dire need at the time – such as when President de Gaulle demanded the U.S. withdraw its troops from France during the Kennedy Administration.

Ed. Note: *JFK's Secretary of State Dean Rusk, in one of his finest hours, asked de Gaulle if that troop pullout also should include the tens of thousands of American soldiers buried in France. Mon General's French detractors often called him "gaulle," which in French slang can mean "dumb."*

...you concentrated on the "positive" aspects of those reports by liberal American journalists who accompanied President Nixon on his historic trip to China, which included the absence of beggars in the streets, elimination of crime, environmental benefits of bicycle travel, etc. Never was it mentioned that this same regime was responsible for the deaths of an estimated 65 million Chinese.

Ed. Note: *Did anyone believe for one minute that the Chinese would allow their visitors from the West to see anything disparaging? The disingenuousness of the American liberal media is as staggering as it is shameful.*

...you agree with Fox News' Alan Colmes and sundry other hand-wringing ninnies that the U.S. should have signed the Kyoto Accord, which even the U.S. Congress rejected overwhelmingly (95-0) as not being in America's best interests; that, in effect, it would cripple our economy while imposing virtually no new environmental limits on certain select countries.

Ed. Note: *Of course, there are those "Americans" who do not place American interests first. But if the senate voted it down unanimously, then it must be unbelievably bad.*

-❧ ✻ ❧-

...you go along with the argument *against* cracking down on illegal immigration across our southern border – terrorism notwithstanding – because it would dry up the cheap labor source needed for crop harvesting and other low-paying jobs which Americans will not accept.

Ed. Note: *Iowa has relatively few foreign-born residents, yet there are plenty of "Iowans" working in agriculture, the hotel industry and fast food businesses, jobs often held elsewhere by illegal immigrants.*

-❧ ✻ ❧-

...it didn't frustrate you that some U.S. liberals always countered any Soviet misadventures (no matter how egregious) by claiming that the U.S. itself had not been perfect in its conduct of international affairs, and therefore a moral equivalency existed.

Ed. Note: *Even after the Soviets unconscionably shot down KAL Flight 007, some liberals claimed it was really a thinly disguised intelligence-gathering mission, operating at least in part under the auspices of the CIA. Not surprisingly, the Soviets agreed.*

...you agree that political pundit Ted Turner (the former Mr. Jane Fonda), hit the nail right on the head as he described the new Soviet premier Mikhail Gorbachev as having "moved more quickly than any person in this history of the world. Moving faster than Jesus Christ did. American is always lagging six months behind."

Ed. Note: *Comment is withheld due to lack of understanding what was said.*

...you were one of those who railed against the first Gulf War in 1991 – even though the UN approved it – and after its successful outcome demanded that Bush (41) stop our troops from going into Baghdad for the *coup de grace*. Of course, after 9/11 happened, you complained that the Republican president didn't finish off Saddam when he had the chance.

…you don't think it strange at all that so many liberals, when referring to Fulgencio Batista, the man deposed by Fidel Castro, use the term "dictator," but never think to call Castro anything but "president."

Ed. Note: *So what? Don't all "presidents" serve 46 year-terms (and still counting) without holding an election? It's good to be president!*

-≒ ✹ ⊨-

…former U.S. Attorney General Ramsey Clark earned your admiration in the early 1990s, when he issued a report accusing the U.S. of "war crimes" – against *Iraq*, which had earlier been thwarted from its barbaric and unprovoked takeover of Kuwait by an American-led coalition.

Ed. Note: *Never one to let his admirers down, Clark later would volunteer to represent Saddam Hussein after the Butcher of Baghdad's capture. Apparently aware of the effectiveness of Clark's track record, Saddam declined the offer.*

-≒ ✹ ⊨-

…in today's war on terrorism, you're more likely to align yourself with those European nations (and the UN) that preach a more understanding attitude and passive response, completely forgetting the lessons learned from the European appeasement of the Nazis.

-≒ ✹ ⊨-

...you can only compare the U.S. invasion of Grenada in 1983 to the Soviets in Afghanistan or the Japanese attack on Pearl Harbor, ignoring that 1,000 Americans – 700 of them medical students – were living on Grenada and were at risk due to a Communist and Cuban takeover.

Ed. Note: *In mounting the invasion, the Reagan administration responded to the urgent request from six Caribbean nations.*

⊰ ❋ ⊱

...during any controversy or confrontation with another nation or adversary, you invariably come down on the side of America's opposition.

⊰ ❋ ⊱

...it never bothered you that Massachusetts Democrat Tip O'Neill Jr. openly admitted that while he was Speaker of the House, he got his "briefings" on Central America from a bunch of activist priests and nuns who did much to shape his views.

Ed. Note: *So much for the congressman's well-paid professional staff, not to mention the nation's intelligence services.*

⊰ ❋ ⊱

...former Washington Post editor Robert Kaiser's article about Finland's womb-to-tomb welfare system – "If We're So Rich and Smart, Why Aren't We More Like Them?" – made a lot of sense to you.

Ed. Note: *It probably never would occur to a liberal that one of the reasons we are so rich and smart is because <u>we aren't at all like</u> the over-taxed, over-governed, under-motivated and uninspired Finns.*

⚔ ✸ ⚔

...you applauded the international crackdown on the use of DDT, proven a highly effective control over malaria worldwide, after Rachel Carson in *Silent Spring* opined that it "may seriously affect reproduction" of quail. Carson's charges were based on an obscure journal article that actually suggested the pesticide helped more than it hurt birds. But after CBS did a special on DDT, thanks to Carson's highly selective reporting, the die had been cast and DDT was on the way out.

Ed. Note: *Almost immediately, the rate of malaria and other mosquito-borne diseases around the globe began to return to their pre-DDT era. Untold numbers died because of a questionable three-percent reduction in quail births.*

⚔ ✸ ⚔

...you're shocked that, while the U.S. is the world's leading producer of carbon dioxide – which *everyone knows* causes global warming – it is doing nothing to mitigate the situation.

Ed. Note: *Two things here: First, nobody yet knows honest-to-god-for-sure if carbon dioxide affects temperatures; and second, nobody knows h-t-g-f-s if global* *warming is for real. If carbon dioxide levels continue to rise exponentially, why has the average world temperature gone up only about 1 degree Fahrenheit in the last 100 years?*

Liberal Lollygagging

"Then the idiot who praises with enthusiastic tone, all centuries but this and every country but his own"

-- Gilbert and Sullivan, The Mikado

Everybody knows "lollygagging" means to waste time, to deal in trivialities, particularly when more important and more meaningful actions are called for (Quit your lollygagging!). The practice becomes insidious when we intentionally do the *glossy* thing that looks good on the surface – possibly because it's fun and easy to do – but ignore the more difficult, more substantive, since that doesn't add readily to our perceived brilliance; and it may even be boring.

Most of us lollygag from time to time. Usually it's a fairly innocuous practice as long as we keep it confined to life's more trivial matters. You might do the *l-word* at a buddy's house because you know if you go home too early, someone will expect you to perform some task you won't like doing right then – such as washing the family car. No big deal, you can wash the car tomorrow. No one gets hurt.

On the other hand, people should not lollygag when time might be of the essence or a critical matter is involved. We may sense something is seriously wrong with our health and it's getting worse. Perhaps we have a family history of some chronic malady, but we've always been the *rugged individualist.* On top of that, we "hate" going to the doctor (most men do, studies tell us). But this is no time to lollygag. Sometimes procrastination kills.

America finds itself in a position today in the world where it simply cannot deal in lollygagging. Knowing what we know now about special conflicts of interest (speaking euphemistically) the French and Russians had with Iraq prior to the coalition invasion, can any reasonable person honestly believe we would have gained anything by sitting around and talking the problem to death (lollygagging) at the U.N.? Remember, our French and Russian allies are Security Council members.

Yet, that's what John Kerry and John Edwards, Howard Dean, Teddy Kennedy, Nancy Pelosi, most of the liberal media, and a host of Hollywood luminaries would have had us do. That's what liberals do.

That's what Neville Chamberlain and a whole British people (excepting Churchill) did in the 30s with Hitler. It's pretty much what the Clinton administration did after the first World Trade Center bombing in the 90s. And it's what a good part of Europe is doing today with terrorism. In all cases, *lollygagging was* not the proper response, if a response at all. In all cases, those engaging in it paid the price – or will.

Perhaps a bit shopworn, but no less true and timely, was this warning posted by the anti-Nazi German Pastor Martin Niemöller:

> *"First they came for the Jews and I did not speak out – because I was not a Jew. Then they came for the communists and I did not speak out -- because I was not a communist. Then they came for the trade unionists and I did not speak out – because I was not a trade unionist. Then they came for me – and by then there was no one left to speak out for me."*

Sir Winston Churchill phrased it with the same foreboding, though more trenchant, when he said *appeasement* does nothing more than demonstrate your hope that the crocodile will eat you last. Talking a problem to death to the exclusion of action…or refusing to speak out against it…or pacifying the perpetrator, all take up residence in the Land of Lollygag.

The Iraqi war opponents still gravely intone it's *the wrong war in the wrong place at the wrong time.* There were no WMDs and there was no connection between Saddam Hussein and Osama bin Laden. What if that were true? It's not. But what if it were?

The fact is, in the horrific aftermath of 9/11 there existed an undeniable blood lust across the land. Americans could taste revenge. We wanted it badly. Yet, we were told we faced an unconventional enemy, one that did not have a native homeland – unlike the Nazis or the "Japs" of 60 years earlier. So exactly who is it we stick it to?

Perhaps Baghdad *did not* qualify ideally for that dubious homeland distinction. Yet Iraq was a rogue state, for years in blatant defiance of the *capons* at the UN, who acted with their traditional decisiveness and clarity of purpose to bring Saddam Hussein to heel. Also, Iraq was, without a doubt, responsible for encouraging and bankrolling terrorism aimed at the Israelis – by Hussein's own admission.

Further, Saddam would no doubt be a free man living *somewhere* today – Syria or maybe even France – and his sons alive, had he heeded the president's ultimatum to "get out of Dodge." He chose to trust French assurances that he was safe, that Jacques Chirac's people at the United Nations would handle it. The French did not. The UN did not. George Bush and the U.S. did.

Here's the bottom line: *The Iraqi war did not have to happen – and would not have – but for France's interference and intransigence.* Certainly that fact has not escaped people. You can bet it hasn't escaped Hussein. Maybe people just forgot the unraveling of events leading up to the war. Oh, look, there's another *cochons volent*!

If most Americans were honest about it, they would admit to having felt some satisfaction when we put the screws to the Butcher of Baghdad. Not by anyone's lights could he have been regarded as a figure of pity or pathos. In lieu of a Berlin or Tokyo, Baghdad stood as the next best target. Iraq openly supported terrorism (proudly, in fact), had used WMDs in the past on its own people and against Iran, fomented two wars in the region, and continued for several years in defiance of UN resolutions – all the time making billions of illegal dollars off the Oil for Food program. Even that last might have been understandable were he using the money to make a better life for Iraqis. But we now know it went into more weaponry and otherwise into Saddam's personal coffers. – while much of Baghdad continued to suffer inadequate power and other basic infrastructure woes.

Some might argue that Tehran or Damascus should have been our target, but it's doubtful the outcome would have been much different than what it is today in Baghdad; and if there was one SOB in the Middle East who most deserved removal, it was Hussein.

Thanks to the war on Iraq, Americans felt at least a little less frustrated over the horrors caused by a *faceless nation attacking us*. We also experienced a bit of recouped pride after being devastated by a small group of pug-ugly ne'er-do-wells who delivered such a stunning blow to our national self-image. To sum it up, *revenge* – which ain't nothin' to be ashamed of.

Under certain circumstances, lollygagging (which began this harangue) strongly suggests a *cowardly character* – the lack of inner strength to face matters when they should be confronted squarely, whether domestic or across the pond. A similar tactic involves responding to those problems by throwing money at them – as liberals did with North Korea, and would have us do today with Iran. Just buy them off as you would any bully on the playground. Everybody knows how that scenario plays out.

No question about it: It's tough playing hardball under high-stakes circumstances. If it weren't, there would be no problems because everybody would be doing it right – the first time. On the other hand, what are the alternatives?

We can't continue to *buy* time interminably, because soon enough the currency we're using will be worthless. If Pastor Neimöller were alive today, he'd agree.

...you believe that everybody in the world is at heart a decent person, who is either misunderstood or compelled to act unconscionably by outside forces – which prompts your apologies for the French and other so-called allies in the 21st Century.

※

...your knee jerks every time the subject of gun control comes up, even with the results of a 2003 study by the U.S. Center for Disease Control and Prevention, which found no link between gun control laws and lower crime rates.

Ed. Note: *The study noted "insufficient evidence to determine the effectiveness of any of the firearms laws or combinations of laws reviewed on violent outcomes." In two states – Texas and Florida – where it became easier for law-abiding citizens to carry guns, homicide rates dropped by 60 percent in four years (Texas) and 23 percent in five years (Florida).*

※

...shortly after 9/11, you agreed with those who suggested the blame for that tragedy lay with the Bush administration – in power for *eight months* at the time of the attack. Particularly at fault, they claimed, was the American intelligence community.

Ed. Note: *The detractors "failed to remember" that both the Carter and Clinton administrations seriously gutted America's intelligence operations; that liberal* *legislators hamstrung the CIA and FBI when it came to sharing information; and that President Clinton did nothing substantive after the first WTC attack (to the dismay of some of his staff), but treated it more as a civil crime than an act of terrorism.*

-≡ ✵ ≡-

...you come from a family with ties to the Eastern Establishment, whose members boast *given* names such as Madison, Haley, Chase or Bailey (and that includes the men) – most of whom serve in the State Department or Foreign Service. At least *mumsie* is proud.

-≡ ✵ ≡-

...suddenly you become *fiscally responsible* when it comes time to defend America in the wake of 9/11; especially in view of your associates' long history of monumental taxing and spending for domestic welfare (aka "entitlement") programs.

-≡ ✵ ≡-

...you're in the scant 56 percent of those self-anointed liberals polled in 2003 by Gallup, who said they were proud of their country – as opposed to the 80 percent of self-described conservatives in the same poll, who expressed their pride in America.

Ed. Note: *Sounds like two different countries*

-≡ ✵ ≡-

...the call by some leading Democrats in Congress for the dilution or outright dissolution of America's Patriot Act and other security measures in place as a result of 9/11, do not trouble you.

Ed. Note: *Though periodic terrorist outbursts, such as the London bombing in July 2005, do give even liberals pause for thought occasionally.*

❧ ✳ ❧

...you agree with Democrats that U.S. intelligence let America down both before and after 9/11, but seem to forget that Bill Clinton took a page from Jimmy Carter's presidency when he all but dismantled our intelligence community during the 1990s.

❧ ✳ ❧

...to you, Jimmy Carter's escalating number of homilies regarding American foreign policy and everything else – now that he's out of office – ring every bit as *astute and relevant* as when he served in the White House.

Ed. Note: *Too bad the American body politic didn't agree with you, handing Carter the worst defeat ever suffered by an incumbent president. He won six states.*

❧ ✳ ❧

...you're thrilled every time you hear the use of "quagmire" by Democrats to describe (a) the pre-war; (b) the war; and (c) the war's aftermath in Iraq.

Ed. Note: *"Quagmire" more appropriately refers to wet, spongy, slushy or muddy earth, not too much of which even liberals can find in the desert. Not to be confused with muckraking, which is pretty much a liberal universal found everywhere.*

⚜

...the exploits of Oscar winner Sean Penn thrilled you as he took a well-orchestrated fact-finding tour of Baghdad, conducted by members of the Iraqi regime prior to the coalition invasion – which seemingly convinced Penn that "the blood of Americans and Iraqis alike will be on our hands."

Ed. Note: *Say what? Penn later admitted the Iraqis had used him as a propaganda tool.*

⚜

...you feel that most anyone who's "rich," either inherited his wealth (which probably makes him unworthy of it), or stole it from the more deserving, which means it should be redistributed among the "have-nots" via burdensome taxes and enervating welfare programs.

Ed. Note: *Actually, Teddy Kennedy deserves a special place here: He inherited his wealth from a father who made much of his fortune from bootlegging. Other than that, Teddy has had to live on a senator's stipend.*

⚜

...like Howard Dean, you're more concerned about surface appearances than you are substance, more preoccupied with process than results. At a time when we might be fighting for our very existence, Dean (and you) would have us sit around and try to talk our way to a solution.

-¤ ✳ ¤-

...your reaction after the smoke barely had cleared from 9/11 was to ask yourself and your fellow Americans, "How were we to blame for making these poor wretches hate us so?"

-¤ ✳ ¤-

...you felt uplifted and righteous to be an American only three days after 9/11, when liberal demonstrators took to the streets in Washington, D.C., displaying placards that urged the U.S. not to respond in kind to those responsible for the terrorism.

-¤ ✳ ¤-

..."profiling" of passengers at American airports is repugnant to you because it means an individual is being singled out mostly because of the way he looks.
Ed. Note: *That then beggars the question: Should an individual be singled out because of the way he doesn't look?*

-¤ ✳ ¤-

...you stick to your claim of revulsion over the concept of profiling at our airports, even after you learn that Arabs have committed 100 percent of all successful terrorist attacks on U.S. commercial flights for the past 20 years.

Ed. Note: *Not only that: It's not politically correct (not to mention un-American) to go around stereotyping people.*

-◄ ✳ ►-

...you're claiming, along with your memory-challenged buddies, that you were all *Cold War Warriors* before the demise of the Soviet Union, when in fact, even today you're first and foremost an America basher.

Ed. Note: *Interesting how some leopards try to change their spots when it seems advantageous to do so, e.g., the "Johns" – Kerry and Edwards*

-◄ ✳ ►-

...it doesn't seem to bother you when you hear the ACLU has been defending the North American Man Boy Love Association (NAMBLA), an organization of pedophiles, which has its own website and now, apparently, its own legal firm.

Ed. Note: *And the madness continues.*

-◄ ✳ ►-

...you've been strangely quiescent about America's sieve-like southern border and a U.S. policy that doesn't display any sense of urgency or concern over the hemorrhaging of illegals into the states; any number of whom could be terrorists disguised as farm laborers or other Mexican job seekers

Ed. Note: *Shame on both parties, which are battling for the Spanish-speaking vote. If* **you** *were a terrorist bent on violent subversion in the U.S., can you think of a surer way to get into this country? C'mmmon!*

⊰ ❋ ⊱

...it took a decision by the U.S. Supreme Court – that confiscated an individual's property in Virginia and handed it over to a private commercial developer – before you were finally convinced that American courts are not supposed to be in the business of making laws.

Ed. Note: *It marked one of the few times since 9/11 that television news viewers actually saw Democrats and Republican members of congress stand up and speak from the same page.*

⊰ ❋ ⊱

...you agree that America should not be so dependent on Middle East oil – especially in time of war – yet you cave in every time to the pseudoscientific environmentalists, the animal rights extremists, and the Blame America First crowd, all of whom scream bloody murder at any hint of our exploiting U.S. domestic oil reserves.

Ed. Note: *Now at all time highs, how much more costly will Middle East oil have to get before someone begins*

displaying some sanity and a well-equipped codpiece in order to do what is clearly the correct and proper thing.

⊰ ❋ ⊱

...you can square liberals' incessant drum beating for improved security measures at this nation's airports, seaports and sundry other transportation terminals on the one hand, with their equally strong determination to dismantle the Patriot Act on the other.

Ed. Note: *Yeah, what's up with that?*

⊰ ❋ ⊱

...that preeminent soothsayer Al Gore caught your fancy when, in deriding Ronald Reagan's Strategic Defense Initiative (aka "Star Wars"), he said, "The Soviets have always found the rubles to match our military escalation...to assume that they're the ones who would buckle is madness."

Ed. Note: *File that in the "Words You Wish You Could Take Back" drawer. Oh, and order up a cup of "madness" for Mr. Gore.*

⊰ ❋ ⊱

...you believed the arguments of "Star Wars" opponents that, on the one hand SDI was a fantasy, which never would work, but that it also would be dangerous and destabilizing. You never asked how it could not work –

which the Soviets would have known – yet be dangerous at the same time.

Ed. Note: *Anatoly Dobrynin, former Soviet ambassador to the U.S., would later claim the Soviets saw SDI as a bona fide threat because they were convinced superior U.S. technology knew something they didn't. Then again, what does he know?*

❈

...you sloughed off the fact that the National Organization for Women (NOW) objected to calling the Laci Peterson tragedy a double-murder case, since it wasn't possible to determine whether the little *entity* that washed ashore in California was "born or unborn."

Ed. Note: *Of course, many of these same activists will demonstrate in a "death watch" for hours outside a prison, protesting the execution of a convicted murdered such as Scott Peterson – ironically.*

❈

...it doesn't seem to you that the feminist movement has gone just a little bit goofy, as epitomized by Libbie Hubbard, a graduate student addressing a U. of Massachusetts rally, who critiqued campus architecture: "...take a look at the buildings around this campus. There's a penis in the center of campus. The library is a giant dick. We must tear it down and get back to the ovum. We have to start constructing buildings in the side of hills so they look like vaginas."

Ed. Note: *One can only wonder the mental state some walk around in that inspires them to see every edifice in terms of its resemblance to a sexual organ. Someone get Architectural Digest on the phone.*

※

...your concern for the rights of a criminal, often a recidivist, frequently outweighs your concern for the victim.

Ed. Note: *It is terribly sad that victims of crime in this country often feel both the criminal and the judicial system have victimized them, because activist judges, flying in the face of common sense, fail to mete out proper punishment.*

※

...your mantra is, "the law is the law," regardless how nonsensical and counterproductive, such as when an order of nuns attempted to convert an abandoned building in the South Bronx into a homeless shelter for dozens of men. After two years of wrangling with New York building authorities, they were told the code required installation of an elevator at a cost of another $100,000.

Ed. Note: *The nuns abandoned the project, feeling they could better use that money and the original $500,000 they had set aside for reconstruction to buy the homeless soup and sandwiches. The fact that the nuns' ascetic beliefs prohibited them from using an elevator did not sway the authorities.*

Media Miscreants

"It's the responsibility of the media to look at the president with a microscope, but they go too far when they use a proctoscope."

-- Richard M. Nixon

If you find the liberal news media particularly fascinating – as do I being an on-again/off-again journalist – you would do well to read veteran reporter Bernard Goldberg's two excellent books, *Bias* and *Arrogance*. Goldberg makes an interesting case for members of the liberal media who believe they and their friends are *middle-of-the-road*. That was how CBS's Dan Rather once proclaimed the Op-ed page of the *New York Times* to Bernie Goldberg: *middle-of-the-road*. That would be laughable, were it not so duplicitous.

But Goldberg contends members of the liberal media are tendentiously insular when it comes to working, hobnobbing, and otherwise interfacing with other sentient beings. Everybody they know and care about happens to be of the same political stripe. They think, therefore, they pretty much share a political philosophy with the great American proletariat, including those in the so-called fly-over red states.

Pauline Kael, an astute film critic for the *New Yorker* 30-plus years ago, simply could not believe that Richard Nixon whomped George McGovern for the Presidency in 1972, even though Nixon won all but one state. Kael could only lament, "Nobody I know voted for Nixon."

The sad thing is, the poor woman probably was telling the truth.

If anyone doubts there's a double standard existing among elitist (aka *liberal)* media, refer them to the Juanita Broaddrick case. The Bush "memogate" fiasco of last election year aside, it's too bad Dan Rather never will have to answer for any of his other less than savory professional practices. Journalistically speaking, many of them were unforgivable sins of omission when it came to liberal peccadilloes or worse.

Classic case in point was when Juanita Broaddrick charged Bill Clinton with having raped her. By all accounts she was a very credible witness. Polls said 80 percent of respondents who heard her allegations thought they were either "true" or "possibly true." Yet Dan Rather failed to mention those allegations – even once – on his *CBS Evening News.* The story might as well not have existed. Rather's later explanation was that he did not report the episode out of respect for the president's "private sex life" – another noble liberal gesture. Would a florist's private sex life, or that of a barber, or a cabdriver been fair game? Since when does a "rape" charge constitute someone's private sex life – which should be protected?

Now ask yourself, knowing what you know about Rather's past performance in "memogate:" If George Walker Bush were charged with rape, instead of William

Jefferson Clinton, would Dan Rather have acted so benignly in refusing to report credible rape charges against a sitting president of the United States – *out of respect for that president's "private sex life*?" The blood roils and boils.

Even Bill Clinton on occasion has described the media as "the knee-jerk liberal press."

The American television media present a conundrum all their own: Supposedly always sensitive to their demographics, the big three networks tend to act differently when it concerns feature news shows, e.g. *48 Hours, Dateline, 20/20*, as they relate to people *of color* or *ethnicity*; because their "numbers" (whether correct or not) tell them most of the predominantly white viewing audience for such shows just doesn't care that much about such stories.

As one NBC News correspondent reportedly confessed, "Let's not kid ourselves, these shows make a tremendous amount of money. There's no profit in people of color." By the way, that's one of the very few times we will hear the liberal media talk in conciliatory terms about the profit motive in business.

Yet, when it comes to their general news reporting, the networks stick to what is clearly a liberal bias – even though an annual Gallup Poll for the last three or four years has revealed that 40 percent of their viewers consider themselves *conservative;* another 20 percent say they're *independent* or *middle-of-the-road*; and the remainder call themselves *liberal* – except, perhaps, for those who have adopted the *progressive* appellation.

Go figure.

Check it out: L. Brent Bozell III, founder and president of The Media Research Center, has written the definitive work on the subject thus far: *Weapons of Mass Distortion – The Coming Meltdown of the Liberal Media* (Crown Forum, New York, 2004)

...you were properly elated when the Associated Press called Florida *for* vice president Gore in the 2000 presidential election, even though, as we later learned, its own numbers showed Bush ahead.

Ed. Note: *The AP further exacerbated its gaffe later that election night when it failed to reverse its call in timely fashion, even after its own numbers and those of other news services showed Bush the actual winner in Florida. The "premature" call by the AP also disenfranchised several thousand voters (mainly from Florida Republican strongholds,) who did not show up to vote because the AP and the networks reported the outcome already had been decided*

❈

...it troubled you not a bit that *Newsweek*, which had a tape of Monica Lewinsky discussing her "affair" with a president of the United States, decided not to use the story. After all, wouldn't the magazine have given George Bush the same pass under similar circumstances?

Ed. Note: *Most American forget that the Lewinsky story broke on the Internet thanks to Matt Drudge ("The Drudge Report").*

❈

...you had no trouble understanding Dan Rather's logic when he begrudgingly, and belatedly, acknowledged that negative memos about George W. Bush's National

Guard service were "probably" bogus – but then maintained that the story was accurate anyway.

Ed. Note: *All this after the network's own experts refused to authenticate the documents, and their "unimpeachable source" turned out to have a long history of George Bush hating. For Dan Rather, it was the classic example of "wanting something too much."*

⟻ ❋ ⟼

...righteously you applaud the *New York Times* for pursuing an aggressive policy of ethnic and gender diversity among its newsroom staff, which *The Gray Lady* herself points to with justifiable pride.

Ed. Note: *Would that such diversity could be found in the newspaper's editorial policies and general journalistic ethos.*

⟻ ❋ ⟼

...you agree with Dan Rather and the *NewYork Times* that the newspaper is truly middle-of-the-road, even though it hasn't endorsed a Republican presidential candidate since Dwight D. Eisenhower in the 1950s.

Ed. Note: *Let's not overlook the good things to be said for consistency.*

⟻ ❋ ⟼

...the always intrepid *Washington Post* lifted your spirits when it withdrew its support for the Pentagon's

Freedom Walk planned in memory of those killed on 9/11. Instead of donating public service advertising space to help promote the march and its Clint Black concert as planned, the newspaper will make a contribution to the Pentagon Memorial Fund.

Ed. Note: *The Post, bowing to pressures from "peace activists" and its own staffers, said it feared that its original plans supporting the march might lead readers to question its objectivity. Sounds a little like the United Nations allowing 800,000 Africans to be slaughtered in Rwanda because it did not want to be seen taking sides.*

⚜

...you disagree with Dick Morris, former campaign manager to President Clinton, who has said the "(New York) *Times* puts its polls, its editorials, and its front page to work, marshaling one strategy after another to regain the momentum the left lost after September 11."

Ed. Note: *Morris and others have charged that the Gray Lady also manipulates her public opinion polls in order to slant their outcomes and advance the newspaper's leftist point of view.*

⚜

...it was with great anticipation that you awaited the major impact to be made on the American political scene by the spate of new liberal radio talk shows that began appearing with the idea of neutralizing conservative talk radio – including those shows hosted by such liberal notables as Mario Cuomo, Jerry Brown and Alan Dershowitz.

Ed. Note: *All failed, rather miserably, as did shows hosted by Gary Hart, Ed Koch, Lowell Weicker, Jim Hightower and Douglas Wilder, liberals all.*

⊷ ❈ ⊶

…you were appalled when media reports came in from Baghdad that more than 170,000 artifacts, many of them priceless, were reportedly stolen from the National Museum of Iraq in the aftermath of the war. How could the U.S. military satisfactorily protect the Ministry of Oil but not this repository of civilization, asked ABC's Peter Jennings? A few days later, Jennings had to admit it appeared that only 27 "significant pieces" were apparently stolen.

Ed.Note: *Though apparently he felt compelled to blame the military for the filching fantasy, Jennings saw no reason to apologize when the museum curator set the record straight.*

⊷ ❈ ⊶

…most mornings you awake with contrition to the hand-wringing, *mea culpa* reports from *CBS News* or the *New York Times*, which suggest Americans are the source of all the planet's ills – a world that would be better off without us.

...you heartily agreed with on-again, off-again TV personality Phil Donahue in his nifty, syllogistic reasoning about patriotism. He called it "the last refuge of scoundrels" and cautioned his viewers, "Beware of patriotism."

Ed. Note: *Donahue may have purloined that "scoundrel" thing from someone famous. In any case, you have been properly warned.*

--- ❋ ---

...you honestly believe the following current television news reporters are the objective professionals their networks purport them to be (their previous employers are listed in parenthesis): ABC's George Stephanopoulos (Bill Clinton); CNN's Jeff Greenfield (Bobby Kennedy); NBC's Tim Russert (Daniel Patrick Moynihan); MSNBC's Chris Mathews (Jimmy Carter); PBS's recently-retired Bill Moyers (Lyndon Johnson).

Ed. Note: *This represents only a very partial list.*

--- ❋ ---

...the irony escapes you that those "mainstream" journalists who try to eviscerate Rush Limbaugh at every turn, never even would have heard of Limbaugh if they had performed their jobs in a less biased fashion.

--- ❋ ---

...you don't subscribe to the hogwash that the "mainstream media" display any liberal bias, notwithstanding that nearly 90 percent of the Washington, D.C. media polled in 2004 voted for John Kerry.

Ed. Note: *Same election: Less than 50 percent of American voters nationwide cast their ballots for Kerry.*

⊣ ❋ ⊢

...you become unhinged over those who describe as "left-wing," such middle-of-the-road publications as the *New York Times* and the *Washington Post*.

Ed. Note: *In 1984, both newspapers endorsed Walter Mondale for president over incumbent Ronald Reagan. Reagan won the popular vote in 49 of 50 states that year.*

⊣ ❋ ⊢

...when the *New York Times* disingenuously referred to the terrorist butcher Abu Musab al-Zarqawi in a July 2005 news story as a "Jordanian fighter," it didn't raise any hackles on you.

Ed. Note: *Arguably, "The Gray Lady" and other mainstream media have called George W. Bush worse.*

⊣ ❋ ⊢

...you thought it not strange at all that ABC would give Vladimir Pozner, a spokesman in the employ of the Soviet Union at the time, an eight-minute, uninterrupted televised rebuttal immediately following a speech by President Reagan.

Ed. Note: *Today, that equates with Rush Limbaugh appearing on Russian network TV following an address by Vladimir Putin. Except that Limbaugh is not a U.S. government employee. ABC later apologized after the White House complained, suggesting the move was ill conceived to begin with.*

⊰ ✳ ⊱

...the irony escaped you when CBS announced it was studying a "story-telling" format for its *new* Evening News show in the wake of Dan Rather's semi-retirement. Wait, does that mean the network is bringing Rather back?

Ed. Note: *Thanks again to Jay Leno.*

⊰ ✳ ⊱

...you, along with CNN's Wolf Blitzer, failed to blink in 1999, when presidential candidate Al Gore told Blitzer that "I took the initiative in creating the Internet."

Ed. Note: *No one in the liberal media empire reported the statement for more than a week, knowing it was an outrageous fabrication, which they didn't want attributed to a Democratic presidential contender. But it wouldn't be the first or last time the media failed to report one of Gore's "misspeakings" on the campaign trail.*

By contrast, presidential candidate George Bush couldn't even get away with mispronouncing a word on TV; not even if everyone in Texas pronounced it the same way. That's how he became known as "George Dubya" – for mispronouncing a letter.

❈

...you disagreed with U.N. Ambassador Jane Kirkpatrick, who said at the 1984 Republican National Convention that Reagan's policies were working, and especially when she added, "the Russians had nearly taken over until the Reagan administration."

Ed. Note: *Where had they nearly taken over, demanded New York Times Columnist Flora Lewis: Aden, Afghanistan, Angola, Cambodia, Congo, Ethiopia, Grenada, Laos, Libya, Madagascar, Mozambique, Nicaragua, the Seychelles, South Vietnam and South Yemen, came the alphabetized response – all in the decade before Reagan's inauguration.*

❈

...the words of *TIME* magazine contributor Nina Burleigh best summed it up for you and others in favor of abortion: "I would be happy to give him [Bill Clinton] a blow job just to thank him for keeping abortion legal. I think American women should be lining up with their presidential kneepads on to show their gratitude for keeping the theocracy off our backs."

Ed. Note: *After airing that sentiment, Ms. Burleigh failed to report whether she had been contacted by Bill Clinton – to express his appreciation.*

⊰ ✳ ⊱

...you *tsk, tsk, tsked* all over the place when ABC's *World News Tonight* ran a story on two Afghan civilians who were accidentally killed by a U.S. bombing in Oct. 2001.

Ed. Note: *ABC ran that piece in place of a story that occurred at the same time about Islamic terrorists, who had massacred 16 Christians as they worshipped at a Catholic church in Pakistan.*

⊰ ✳ ⊱

...it phased you not a whit that CBS reporter John Burns exposed that shameful chapter in American journalism, when (overwhelmingly) liberal journalists in Iraq – prior to the second Gulf War – failed to report the horrific atrocities taking place in that country because they feared they might be kicked out by Saddam and no longer able to report.

Ed. Note: *Report what?*

⊰ ✳ ⊱

...you related to the Washington. D.C. peace marchers in January 2003 – whom, the media told us, were Republicans, honor students, grandparents, the ubiquitous soccer moms, veterans, you name it – gathered to protest a possible war in Iraq. The elitist media did not report, and you did not care, that the march was organized by a far left group called ANSWER (Act Now to Stop War and End Racism).

Ed. Note: *ANSWER's charter members' roster reads like a who's who of America and Bush haters, including Ramsey Clark, Janeane Garofalo, Michael Moore and Jessica Lange.*

⚜

...National Public Radio (NPR), which is funded by taxpayers, did the right thing as far as you're concerned when it admitted its priority was reporting the locations of the U.S. military in Afghanistan, even if that meant putting American troops at risk.

Ed. Note: *Perhaps someone at NPR remembered its funding sources, because several weeks later it finally vouchsafed a clarification, disavowing its previous statement.*

⚜

...the relative ease with which U.S.-led coalition troops dispatched the Iraqis caused you to agree with many news media that the U.S. might be seen by other nations as a bully; that included *U.S. News & World Report, Newsweek* and *ABC*.

Ed. Note: *Just days earlier, the same media had speculated that we were bogged down in another*

Vietnam quagmire, some saying that the American war plan had failed.

...the gushing reports by liberal media people concerning the newly elected Mikhail Gorbachev gave you hope. *CBS's* Dan Rather said Gorbachev had "impressive eyes...the look of a human volcano;" Mary McGrory of the *Washington Post* said he "had a blueprint for saving the planet." Author Gail Sheehy commented on Grobachev's "luminous presence."

Ed. Note: *By contrast, Ronald Reagan was still just a "cowboy," according to the American liberal press. How could he stand up to such a formidable foe as "Gorby?"*

...you were upset that Congress cut funding for the Public Broadcasting System in 2005, citing PBS's overwhelming political bias in its liberal programming that has cost American taxpayers more than $7 billion since 1967.

Ed. Note: *To stave off the funding cuts, PBS used taxpayer monies to produce scare TV commercials that warned viewers its children's programs were in danger of termination as a result of Congressional actions. If there's a cheap shot to be taken, guess who takes it?*

...it surprised you that the *New York Times* did not see fit to publish a financial scandal about liberal radio network Air America until three weeks after it appeared in the *New York Daily News*. Even then, it relegated the story to page 3, inappropriately edited some quotes to change their meaning, neglected to mention "Air America" in the 15-word headline, and misidentified a boys and girls club as the alleged culprit, not the network.

Ed. Note: *All the news that prints to fit, or something like that.*

-¤ ❀ ¤-

...you thought it was funny when CBS TV personality Bryant Gumbel called Robert Knight of the Family Research Council a "fucking idiot," as he left the set, not realizing the cameras were still on. Knight is an advocate for family values, who defended the Boys Scouts of America's decision to ban homosexual troop leaders.

Ed. Note: *Not surprisingly, CBS took no known action against Gumbel. They probably disciplined him by firing the cameraman.*

-¤ ❀ ¤-

...it caught you flatfooted when the Associated Press admitted that it's not covering the Iraqi hostilities as fairly as it could because it unintentionally omits positive progress reports out of concerns for reporters' safety. The story appeared on page 2 of the *New York Times*.

Ed. Note: *An anonymous e-mail to a Tampa newspaper editor tipped her that Americans haven't been told that 47 countries have re-established their embassies in Iraq and that 3,100 schools have been renovated – as examples of what hasn't been reported.*

⊰ ✳ ⊱

…it failed to infuriate you that Reuters wire service, headquartered in London, directed its reporters and editors not to use the term "terrorist" in describing the WTC attacks because, "We all know that one man's terrorist is another man's freedom fighter…"

Ed. Note: *It was this same Reuters that reported the Oklahoma City bombing as a "terrorist attack."*

⊰ ✳ ⊱

…you approved when ABC's Peter Jennings reported on the death of convicted Soviet spy Alger Hiss in 1996, and said Hiss had been exonerated the year before by Russian President Boris Yeltsin, who claimed KGB files supported the man's innocence.

Ed. Note: *The only problem with that fairy tale is that Yeltsin never made such a statement. Russian General Dimitri Volkogonov had announced earlier in a letter that he could find no evidence of Hiss' espionage activities in KGB files. But shortly after, the general admitted that Hiss' attorney John Lowenthal somehow*

101

"pushed me to say things of which I was not fully convinced." Volkogonov confessed he hardly had read any of the files, and that much had been destroyed after Stalin's death anyway. Case closed, already.

-¤ ❋ ¤-

...as far as you're concerned, *Newsweek's* Eleanor Clift nailed it when she described the U.S. military as "a mercenary army." Among her other sterling quotes, Clift said, "...we're basically paying people to serve their country."

Ed. Note: *One wonders what the color of the sky might be in some liberals' worlds. Go back to the American Civil War and you'll learn troops on both sides were being paid. The most basic definition of "mercenary" is one who is paid to serve in a <u>foreign</u> nation's military. Did veteran reporter Clift not bother to look that up?*

Political & Parasitical

"Those who are too smart to be engaged in politics are punished by being governed by those who are dumber."

-- Plato

Where to begin on the subject of American politics? *They stink*, would be a good start. They've never been as *petty, vicious, vitriolic and just plain mean-spirited* as they are today, would be a natural extension of that articulation. What's responsible for this most recent dirtying of an already dirty American institution?

Some people point to two consecutive presidential victories by the Republicans – particularly with George W. Bush as their standard bearer – as the main reason why our politics have hit a new low and polarized voters as dramatically as they have. Those losses did not make liberals happy, especially the first one, over which an amazing number of Democrats still cry *foul*. Losing Congress did not exactly salve liberal wounds either. But even most Beltway liberals confess that their Congressional debacle has been a sorry Clinton legacy more than a Bush victory – that and maybe some gerrymandering tossed in for good measure.

At its most elemental, the elitists among the liberals can't understand how it's possible they could have been defeated by the likes of George W. Bush. The man doesn't even speak English well, they sniff. On election night, John Kerry himself was overheard to *mystify* aloud about, how could he be losing to "such an idiot?" Even the ranking Democrat in the Senate got into the act by telling a bunch of Nevada school kids that their president is a "loser." Then you have a congress*person* from California who runs around Washington every week like some sort of demented Red Queen, screaming "off with his head" – which seems to include most any head not attached to a liberal body.

American politics have been dumbed down to a new low…or, always low American politics have reached new "heights of lowness" – take your pick, they're one and the same. The really tragic part of it is that the public loses big time in the process. Instead of being delivered cogent, rational and clearly stated arguments by its "leadership" in Washington, it's subjected to the most sophomoric distortions, half-truths and outright (and obvious) lies – actually quite insulting to the national intelligence.

A Republican president's chief advisor is accused of leaking the identity of a CIA operative to the media. Before a Grand Jury can even be convened, Democrats are screaming for his ass in a sling, and they continue to scream while evidence is being gathered and secret testimony presented.

Not a day goes by for at least a couple of weeks when some demagogue isn't heard or seen demanding that President Bush keep his earlier promise to fire whomever of his staffers might be responsible. Of course, it might be nice if it were first determined that a crime had been committed. Secondly, the president had said from the outset that any staff member found responsible would be called to "account for" his actions. That *could* mean termination. It also could mean "a trip to the woodshed," or *two years in front of a firing squad.*

On the other hand, a former National Security Advisor to a Democratic president, who also was an advisor to a Democratic presidential candidate at the time of the incident, is caught pilfering classified documents from the National Archives. Before the advent of conservative talk radio and Fox News, the malfeasance hardly would have made it as a blip on the radar screen – as operated by America's mainstream media.

Democrats were conspicuously silent over what appeared to be an egregious security breach at the National Archives – except to question the "timing" of the incident's revelation, calling it a ploy to divert America's attention away from the Iraq war. It seems even when a liberal is caught dead to rights in a criminal act, the opprobrium is directed at someone else.

But, when one really considers it, "Bergergate" makes Watergate look like small potatoes. What was Watergate after all, but a few low-level political thugs breaking into some support offices of the Democratic presidential nominee, looking for possible evidence of leftist ties. The real Watergate crime supposedly was Richard Nixon's alleged plans to engage in a cover-up, which by the way, was just that, *alleged.* Nothing was proved because Nixon wouldn't allow it to go that far, only too painfully aware of what lay in store – innocent or not – as the liberal media circled slowly overhead.

All of it smacks of the worst kind of partisan politics. Not only are liberals lying to the people, they're doing it in the most transparent and clumsy manner imaginable. The American public may not be marked by a preponderance of brain surgeons and rocket scientists (what country is?), but Abraham Lincoln had something to say about *fooling the people.*

More recently, former Georgia Democratic Senator Zell Miller was even more explicit than Lincoln: "The day has passed when you can piss on them [the people] and convince them it's raining," Miller, a no-nonsense patriot, has said. But even though clearly articulated, Zell might have further qualified his statement (as Lincoln did) by allowing that *you can't piss on all of the people all of the time and convince them it's raining.* Clearly, there are those who never will learn – or refuse to – and will opt for their bumbershoots and raincoats at the first droplets.

...you sincerely believe those Democrats in Congress who demanded a timeline for troop withdrawal from Iraq were doing so in the best interests of their country, and not for partisan political purposes.

Ed. Note: *If you were a terrorist/insurgent leader, wouldn't you like to know there's a date set for troop withdrawal? You might even be tempted to cut back on your attacks temporarily to convince the coalition countries that it's safe to turn Iraq over to the Iraqis.*

-≈ ※ ≈-

...you agree with DNC Chairman Howard Dean, who has sagely observed that the GOP membership is mainly white Christian (the suggestion being that there is something exclusionary about that).

Ed. Note: *No mean feat, by the way, in a country whose population is mainly white Christian. Come to think of it, do the Dems number more non-Christian people of color among their membership than they do white Christians? "Conservative Democrat Zell Miller said of Dean, "Clever and glib, but deep this Vermont pond is not."*

-≈ ※ ≈-

...it never occurred to you to question why former Clinton Deputy Attorney General Jamie Gorelick was sitting on the 9/11 Commission, which sought to investigate blame for the World Trade Buildings tragedy. Considering it was *Gorelick* who erected the "wall" before 9/11 that prevented U.S. intelligence and law enforcement agencies from cooperating in the war on terrorism, it was unconscionable that she refused to recuse herself. Under the circumstances, it was particularly galling that she questioned CIA and FBI witnesses before the commission, attempting to assess their pre-9/11 performance.

Ed. Note: *Not only did the commission refuse to reveal the contents of a "scathing" 1995 memo from a New York U.S. Attorney, which warned against Gorelick's wall, but it did not even make mention of the memo in its final report. By virtue of her surname alone, one would think Clinton's former deputy attorney general would be a great addition to the staff of his former vice president.*

⊰ ✻ ⊱

...George Bush's search for Weapons of Mass Destruction (including nerve gas) in Iraq was a phony excuse for the war, as far as you're concerned. But a few years earlier, you applauded the legitimacy of Bill Clinton's bombing of an alleged nerve gas production plant in Sudan, supposedly funded by Osama bin Laden.

Ed. Note: *Clinton's Secretary of Defense William Cohen later admitted the plant produced medicines and veterinary products, and that no connection existed between the plant, WMDs and bin Laden. In* *the meantime, more Muslims got pissed at the U.S. for destroying a major source of their pharmaceuticals.*

-❈-

…you condemned President Clinton's impeachment proceedings as the result of a "vast right wing conspiracy," a term coined by that unassailable pillar of truth and objectivity, Hillary Clinton, and since widely adopted and quoted *ad nauseam* by liberals of every stripe.

-❈-

…as far as you're concerned, impeachment proceedings were brought against Bill Clinton solely because he couldn't keep the *presidential prerogative* in his pants while in the White House. And you weren't sure his sex life was anybody's business.

Ed. Note: *Which means you ignored charges of (a) obstruction of justice; (b) perjury; and (c) subornation of perjury – for all of which Clinton was indicted. Sex never entered into the charges.*

-❈-

…you righteously buy into the old canard that the Democrats are the *real* party of the people, while Republicans always represent the avaricious rich and powerful. As Ann Coulter points out, liberalism (aka the Democratic party) is a "whimsical luxury of the very rich – and the very poor, both of whom have little stake in society."

-≍ ✳ ≈-

…after 9/11 you decried any efforts to focus undue attention on Islamists entering the country….or to call on U.S. Islamic leaders to denounce the extremists…or to tighten the immigration weak spots that allowed Islamic attackers to enter the U.S., because it was not the politically correct thing to do.

Ed. Note: *Being murdered is preferable to offending someone.*

-≍ ✳ ≈-

…you blinked and did not see President Clinton's *faux* tears demonstration at Commerce Secretary Ron Brown's funeral, just a split-second after the President realized he had been caught on camera laughing with a crony.

-≍ ✳ ≈-

…it's your view that monies spent by the federal government actually belong to the federal government.

-≍ ✳ ≈-

…it satisfied you that the Clinton Justice Department was right in seeking to *disallow* Proposition 209, which Californians successfully voted for to outlaw affirmative action quotas by the government.

Ed. Note: *So much for the Will of the People.*

❈

...a warm, fuzzy glow enveloped you throughout the 1990s, when time and again countless millions of Americans voted on state ballot initiatives – issues ranging from affirmative action to immigration – only to see a handful of activist federal judges unceremoniously nullify their choices.

Ed. Note: *So much for the Will of the People.*

❈

...it wasn't too long after 9/11 that you declared the "honeymoon was over," and set about to fix blame for the attacks – on the Bush administration, of course. Through commissions, reports, memos, investigations, interviews, it was clear that George Bush and his lackeys, including the intelligence community, dropped the ball.

Ed. Note: *While much of the elitist media seemed open to such suggestions, the American public wasn't buying it. Not even when certain Democrats suggested the White House knew something in advance of the attacks.*

❈

...you watched with approval while it really got asinine, and some Congressional commission members took the administration to task for not scrambling fighter jets to shoot down the airliners before they could complete their missions.

Ed. Note: *Can there be any doubt, for any fair-minded person, that the same commission members would have eviscerated the president for acting on impulse – even if he had been correct and saved hundreds of lives by shooting down those planes? It didn't take much to realize that security wasn't the main issue in those hearings.*

-¤ ❀ ¤-

...you applied for citizenship in Hillary Clinton's "Village," which geopolitically, if not geographically, is located just to the left of Reality Way.

-¤ ❀ ¤-

...Hillary Clinton's humanitarianism moved you when she awarded thousands of dollars in contributions (from the New World Foundation, which she chaired) to groups affiliated with the terrorist PLO.

-¤ ❀ ¤-

...you're playing the *disingenuous* card, claiming to believe Sen. Hillary Clinton has reinvented herself as a plausible wartime leader, while knowing full well how quickly that particular leopard will change her spots should she win the presidency in 2008.

-¤ ❀ ¤-

...you shared Democratic leaders' outrage over charges that Bush Senior Advisor Karl Rove leaked a CIA agent's identity to the media and are demanding that he lose his security clearance/step down/be fired/or be forced to listen to the tape of an old Bill Clinton State of the Union Address. It doesn't seem to make any difference that the Grand Jury was still hearing evidence at the time.

Ed. Note: *Whatever the denouement in this story, it's apparent that the American public (absent a few knee-jerk liberals) really doesn't seem to care very much.*

❈

...along with every American liberal on the planet, you were remarkably comfortable with former Clinton National Security Advisor Sandy Berger, who was caught red-handed (and presumably red-faced) stuffing Top Secret memos from the National Archives down his pants and elsewhere.

Ed. Note: *Berger, who claimed he had made a "mistake" in the stuffing incident, was at the time presidential candidate John Kerry's advisor on national security affairs.*

❈

...you were able to keep awake during the gaseous rantings of Strobe Talbott, former deputy secretary of state under Bill Clinton, who throughout the1980s was able to put the USSR into proper perspective for the

113

faithful. The Soviet Union was "stronger and bolder than ever before," he said. "The U.S. must learn to live with parity...the Soviet Union is ready and able to match America in any kind of arms race."

Ed. Note: *One assumes Talbott and Newsweek's Eleanor Clift were unwitting dupes of the same CIA misinformation cabal; but apparently not the only liberals to be so victimized.*

⊰ ❋ ⊱

...you were one of those crying that John Bolton was "damaged goods" and should not be considered for the ambassadorship to the United Nations. Of course, that also makes you one of those who did his best to damage those goods. Live with it!

Ed. Note: *It reminds one of the little boy who killed his parents, then threw himself on the mercy of the court because he was an orphan.*

⊰ ❋ ⊱

...Al Gore, that madcap wit, really scored on your laugh meter when he publicly described a Republican office-seeker's supporters as "the extreme right wing – the extra-chromosome right wing."

Ed. Note: *However, you may be forgiven if you didn't realize the presence of an "extra chromosome" is the birth defect that creates Down's Syndrome. The unfortunates stricken with it used to be called*

114

"mongoloids," which meant they were moderately to severely mentally deficient.

━❈━

...you were surprised that college transcripts for Al Gore and George Bush proved the two were extremely close in their scholastic achievements – Gore at Harvard and Bush at Yale. But that doesn't stop you from thinking Gore is a soaring intellect and Bush a simplistic cowboy.

Ed. Note: *Bush also speaks fluent Spanish and was a U.S. jet fighter pilot. Gore at one time seriously proposed banning the internal combustion engine in America, and had trouble identifying portraits of George Washington and Benjamin Franklin when visiting Thomas Jefferson's Monticello estate. He also was one of the very few American soldiers who returned after less than six months service in Vietnam – and it wasn't because he was wounded.*

━❈━

...hope sprung eternal when you heard Ohio Democrat Paul Hackett had lost (*lost?*) an August 2005 special Congressional election, because Hackett crowed very much like a *ungracious winner*, claiming "no Republican is safe," since he lost by 52-48 percent in a historically Republican district. "We stood tough and put them in their place," he bragged.

Ed. Note: *Advancing again the theory that black is white, the "liberal loser" presumably considered the defeat a moral victory. Ohio Republicans hope Hackett is prescient when he claims "(we) put them in their place." Surely, all Republican candidates would dearly enjoy being put in that "place," which makes them election winners.*

❈

...it was a case of "suspicions confirmed" when CBS and others attempted to drag George Bush's military record through the mud during the 2004 election; but later, you screamed *foul play* when scores of Vietnam vets, many of whom served with John Kerry on swift boats in Vietnam, cast serious doubts on the validity of his self-reported performance during that war.

Ed. Note: *Lt. Commander Grant Hibbard, who was Kerry's commanding officer at the time, expressed strong doubts about the origins and severity of Kerry's first Purple Heart injury, saying he had seen worse wounds caused by "rose thorns."*

❈

...you think lawyers, by virtue of their obvious intelligence and training, should be heavily involved in this country's government – *legislative, judicial and executive.* Since 1981, lawyers have accounted for nearly 50 percent of U.S. Congressional members.

Ed. Note: *Studies have shown that the preponderance of Americans (unless they themselves are attorneys) simply do not trust lawyers and want nothing to do with them – until, unfortunately, they may have to employ one.*

❊

...the incestuous "lobbyist/lawyer" situation in Washington, D.C. doesn't bother you, in that "law firm" and "lobbying firm" are pretty much one and the same in our Nation's Capitol.

Ed. Note: *While apparently no one is doing anything about it, special interest groups (a haven for lobbyist/ lawyers) represent the single most serious threat to the effective and efficient governance of our country – as they spread around virtually uncountable millions attempting to influence legislation. For proof, look no further than the "pork" found in every Congressional bill of some size. Of course, it couldn't happen without the avaricious concurrence of our legislators – currently, 43 percent of them lawyers.*

Presidential Paroxysms

"In 1932, lame duck President Herbert Hoover was so desperate to remain in the White House that he dressed up as Eleanor Roosevelt. When FDR discovered the hoax in 1936, the two men decided to stay together for the sake of the children."

– Johnny Carson

In reply to a media question about whether President Bush lied in his State of the Union address concerning Saddam Hussein's attempt to purchase uranium from Africa, Democratic Senator Bob Graham (Fla.) – a candidate for his party's presidential nomination at the time – said, "I would not use the three-letter word. I would use the five-letter word – deceit."

Objective journalists (come out, come out, wherever you are!) might have asked whether the Senator was having a problem with his counting or his spelling.

If it weren't for the fact that the *Nitwit Nine* were all liberals and running for the Democratic presidential nomination in 2004 (except Al Sharpton, who waddled), the mainstream media would have had a feeding frenzy. Sometimes the contenders looked comically foolish, standing up there *en masse*, all passing themselves off as viable representatives of their party – and one would suppose – the American people. Then they would confirm that foolishness, by opening their mouths, often taking sophomoric potshots at one another in their fevered quests for the political Holy Grail.

Yes indeed, the elitist media would have filleted these presidential hopefuls on looks alone, as is their *modus operandi* – had the candidates been Republicans.

Earlier, on an even more comic scale, it compared with Cold War Warrior Michael Dukakis posing with his little helmeted-head peering out from inside the American tank. Or John Kerry, late in his presidential campaign, trudging through the Ohio woods trying to look like the nimrod he wasn't, and sacrificing the PETA vote in favor of the NRA. It so transparently shouted PHOTO OPP...PHOTO OPP...PHOTO OPP to the exclusion of any truth. Yet no one in the liberal camp seemed embarrassed by that transparency. Or perhaps, they just didn't believe the public was smart enough to catch on.

Somehow liberals always manage to insert themselves into those situations in which they look like they least belong and are most uncomfortable in. Like the poor *mensch* we all know who invariably laughs at the wrong part of the joke, stepping on the punch line; or who snaps his fingers and claps his hands on the wrong beat of the tune – the Steve Martin character in *The Jerk*.

What really was disturbing to many who watched the *Nitwit Nine* debate – but probably only to those who weren't of the liberal persuasion – was the endless fusillade of mean-spirited, cheap shots that these political *un*worthies leveled at a sitting president of the United States. It went far beyond the political rhetoric one expects from the *loyal opposition*. On occasion, it seemed they tried to outdo each other with the poisonous, pernicious overload of their barbs.

Even Democratic Committee National Chairman Terry McAuliffe admitted, "I can tell you the visceral dislike that they [Democratic leaders] have for George Bush and his policies is something I have never seen before." Later that same day, McAuliffe himself would comment regarding Bush's "absolutely ludicrous and insane statements."

Whether engaging in one of their nationally televised debates, appearing as talk show guests, or simply one-on-one with a reporter, the common thread that seemed to run throughout the comments of the *Nitwit Nine* was an obvious vitriol for George W. Bush – politically and personally.

Yet the Republicans seemed mysteriously hesitant to respond to the vituperations until, that is, the candidate field had been narrowed. Once John Kerry was christened the presumptive Democratic standard bearer, we saw the gloves come off. No longer could a Democrat make an outrageous statement about the administration (or the president, personally) without getting it rammed back down his (or her) throat. And, of course, the Republicans began their own offensive against John Kerry.

Democrats and liberals in general, responded in shocked disbelief that Republicans would wage such a *dirty* campaign; that they would go after Kerry's voting record and the general intransigence and indecisiveness displayed throughout his Congressional career. And just as the Democrats had introduced questions and outright accusations about Bush's military career, so too did Republicans bring up some questions, or suggest certain inaccuracies related to Kerry's military service as reported by the Senator. Of course, then the stuff really hit the fan.

Many seasoned political pundits agreed it was the nastiest, dirtiest, most vile presidential campaign in the history of the Republic. At no other time previously did American voters have more fun hating each other.

...during a presidential campaign you actually believed that the #1 and #4 ranked liberal doves in the U.S. Senate had morphed into hawks overnight in order to combat terrorism if they'd won the election.

-◄ ✳ ►-

...you really, really believed that *all nine* of the Democratic candidates for the presidency in 2004 had any business taking up the voters' time.

-◄ ✳ ►-

...it never occurred to you to ask why Democratic "presidential candidate" Rev. Al Sharpton was even running in 2004, since he had no more chance of winning his party's nomination than did the Rev. Jesse Jackson, from whom Sharpton was trying to wrest leadership of the African-American community.

Ed. Note: *Oh! Sometimes one inadvertently answers one's own questions.*

-◄ ✳ ►-

...it didn't seem questionably ethical to you that liberal James Carville, political "king-maker" and former co-host of CNN's *Crossfire*, took a hiatus from his broadcast job to serve as adviser to John Kerry's meandering presidential campaign in 2004 – only to return to the network at the campaign's conclusion.

Ed. Note: *One wonders what liberal reaction would have been to Bill O'Reilly or Sean Hannity temporarily*

*leaving their jobs at Fox News to help re-elect Bush?
Can you say "conflict of interest," boys and girls?
Wouldn't it be something if Carville still had been on
the CNN payroll while working for Kerry? That's too
delicious to properly savor.*

⊣ ❊ ⊢

...the uncanny resemblance between Democratic
presidential candidate Dennis Kucinich and Mad
Magazine's fictional factotum Alfred E. (What Me
Worry?) Neuman, escaped you.

Ed. Note: *The resemblance ended when Alfred E.
Neuman was asked to run in 2004, and he replied
that he did "not want to waste supporters' money on a
frivolous campaign."*

⊣ ❊ ⊢

...it's still difficult to accept that George *Dubya* beat the
Democrats twice – though, at the same time, it appears
the Dems have no one to blame but themselves, refusing
to follow the blueprint for proven success drawn up by
"Centrist" Bill Clinton.

Ed. Note: *Is there some kind of "critical chip" missing
from the thinking processes of these extremist groups'
leaders – left or right – which prevents them from
grasping the reality that most American voters will
not cast their ballots for ideological extremists – left
or right? Even Tony Blair in England had to beat his*

Labor Party senseless until they moved toward the middle of the political spectrum and won.

-= ❋ =-

...it was okay with you that President Clinton appointed failed Democratic presidential hopeful Carol Moseley Braun (2004), former Illinois senator, to the post of ambassador to New Zealand, after she lost her 1998 re-election bid in Illinois; though previously her checkered political career included accusations of campaign finance irregularities and a visit to Nigeria where she defended brutal dictator Sani Abacha (panned even by Democrats).

Ed. Note: *Braun was the only Democrat incumbent to lose in 1998, and the first Illinois Democrat to lose a Senate race in 20 years.*

-= ❋ =-

...you gullibly anticipated Gen. Wesley Clark's every media interview prior to his run (run?) for the presidential nomination in 2004 to learn if (a) he would indeed run; and (b) which party he would embrace.

Ed. Note: *Perhaps feeling too old and hard-bitten to be playing the "coquette" any longer, the general finally announced for the Democrats (since a Republican already was in the White House, dummy!). Prediction: He will reinvent himself for the 2008 race. In fact, at this writing he's taken a job as an analyst on the Fox News Channel.*

...President Clinton hit the proverbial nail right on the head when he cleverly and graciously re-titled Newt Gingrich's "Contract with America," – *Contract on America* – suggesting that Gingrich was playing the role of a mob hitman.

-¤ ❋ ¤-

... President Reagan's approach to the Cold War was so bellicose it was frightening to you, but also so simplistic it was irrelevant.

Ed. Note: *Mutually exclusive or not, it seems to have worked.*

-¤ ❋ ¤-

...you and your friends – as well as Eastern Europeans– all were outraged when President Reagan visited Berlin in 1982 and committed a *Grenzverletzung*, a "border injury." He intentionally took a couple of symbolic steps across the painted borderline at Checkpoint Charlie without first asking the permission demanded.

Ed. Note: *No one was sure at the time just who was more upset by Reagan's prank – the East Germans and the Soviets, or the American liberals. There goes that Wascally Weagan again.*

-¤ ❋ ¤-

...you've labeled George W. Bush *a cowboy* for his military "adventures," but conveniently forgot (along with today's Dems) that Bill Clinton sent American troops to foreign lands *44 times during his eight-year hitch.*

Ed. Note: *In the 45 years prior to Clinton, the American military had been dispatched overseas only eight times.*

-≡ ❋ ⊨-

...you nodded in agreement when Juan Williams of National Public Radio, appearing on Fox News in July 2005, took President Bush to task for not leveling with the American people that the war on terror would be a protracted one.

Ed. Note: *Apparently newsman Williams paid no attention to news media other than his own, or he would have seen, heard and read countless statements by the president, the secretary of state, secretary of defense, national security adviser and an unending collection of administration officials who had been reiterating that very idea since before the invasion of Afghanistan.*

-≡ ❋ ⊨-

...the unrelenting, mean-spirited vilification of President Bush – politically and personally – by the "Nitwit Nine" during the 2004 campaign did not bother you, but a Republican "payback," once the nine had been winnowed down to one candidate, left you outraged over dirty campaign tactics by the Bush camp.

Ed. Note: *And to think it was a Democrat who liked to say, "If you can't stand the heat..."*

...you've labeled George W. Bush *a cowboy* for his military "adventures," but never objected when Bill Clinton ordered a bombing campaign against Serbia for a three-month period in 1999, without the consent of Congress. In fact, the House voted against it. Also, the Serbs never posed a direct threat to the U.S.

Ed. Note: *The only time in our history a president has waged war without formal congressional approval... where was the loyal opposition? The media? The liberals?*

＊

...the accomplishments of Jimmy Carter's presidency (1976-1980) seem a little blurred. They included gutting the CIA...giving away the Panama Canal...tolerating a Soviet arms buildup without responding in kind and the Soviet invasion of Afghanistan...and betrayal of the Shah of Iran – ultimately leading to the taking and holding of 52 innocent American hostages for more than a year.

Ed. Note: *You also may have forgotten that Iranian mullahs released the hostages on the day Ronald Reagan was sworn in as president to succeed Carter. Another great one for symbolism, during the energy crunch, Carter had the White House heat turned down to the point that some of his staffers had to type while wearing gloves.*

＊

...it slipped by you when Jimmy Carter recently resurrected earlier charges that syndicated columnist George Will had stolen Carter's briefing book for debating Ronald Reagan during the 1980 presidential campaign and delivered it to Reagan's camp. That, Carter said, accounted for his truncated presidency. Many years later, he told a Plains, Ga., church congregation that Will subsequently had written him "asking for forgiveness."

Ed. Note: *George Will swears it never happened, that it would have been inappropriate conduct on his part, and that he never wrote Carter asking for forgiveness for something he did not do. President Carter lost 44 of the 50 states in that election, still a dubious record for an incumbent president.*

❈

...you thought John Kerry displayed his usual rapier-like wit on election night 2004, when he remarked that he couldn't believe he was "getting beat by such an idiot," as reported by Evan Thomas of *Newsweek*, hardly a conservative publication.

❈

...that flimsy fantasy still works for you – the one that George W. Bush won the 2000 election by *stealing* the Florida vote – despite the fact that Bush won the state's original vote count, then won the automatic recount, then won the absentee ballot count. And that Al Gore never won a *single* count.

Ed. Note: *Ad Nauseam and still counting.*

⚜

...the scorch marks of George Bush stealing the election from Al Gore in 2000 are seared indelibly into your memory, though Gore also lost Tennessee (his home state); Arkansas (Bill Clinton's home state); and West Virginia (historically a Democratic bastion), any one of which would have won him the presidency.

Ed. Note: *Even Massachusetts Governor Michael Dukakis, who was as "Yankee" as one can get, won the Mountaineer State in 1988.*

⚜

...you took some solace from the fact that Bush won slightly more than 50 percent of the vote in defeating John Kerry, but conveniently forgot that only 43 percent of Americans voted Bill Clinton into office in 1992.

⚜

...presidential candidate Howard Dean, after an ignominious defeat in the Iowa primary, energized you with his rolling-up-the-sleeves diatribe that most non-liberals regarded as *unhinged.*

Ed. Note: *At the same time, you were probably hoping Dean's manservant did not appear on camera to show Dean how to properly roll up his sleeves.*

...you seriously doubted the president's statement that his goal was "to attack Iraq's nuclear, chemical and biological weapons programs and its military capacity to threaten its neighbors." You also waxed incredulous over his remarks that "the international community had little doubt then, and I have no doubt today that, left unchecked, Saddam Hussein will use these terrible weapons again."

Ed. Note: *Oops! Wrong President. Those were Prez Bill Clinton's words in 1998.*

※

...you eagerly awaited the Democrats' immediate, though predictable rebuttal in the news media to President Bush's ill-conceived and reckless statement that, "It sure is a nice day out there today."

Ed. Note: *It was expected that Teddy Kennedy would claim Bush's remarks indicated we were headed for a "quagmire." Nancy Pelosi would demand that somebody (anybody) step down, but not create any environmental damage while doing it; and Al Gore would blame the "nice day" on Bush's refusal to sign the Kyoto Accord, pointing to the early stages of global warming.*

※

...it hurts to think back, that in the last ten U.S. Presidential elections, only three were won by Democrats (two of those by Bill Clinton). Hubert Humphrey got gored by Nixon in 1968; McGovern lost every state but Massachusetts in '72; after winning in '76, Carter endured the worst defeat of any Democratic presidential incumbent in history in '80; in '84, Mondale won only his home state of Minnesota – by less than 5,000 votes; in '88 Dukakis was humiliated by Bush (41); Gore couldn't win his (or Clinton's) home state in 2000. Kerry lost in 2004 in an election that was not nearly as close as the numbers portrayed.

Ed. Note: *It must be somehow significant that the only Democratic presidents elected in the past five decades had both been Southern governors.*

✂ ❋ ✄

…you bought into Democratic vice presidential candidate John Edwards' noble argument in 2004 about all the individual suffering his law firm alleviated by its handling of torts, at the same time sticking it to big business and the medical community in an effort to shape them up.

Ed. Note: *The downside to such activities, which few seem to note, is that the huge awards which juries make to allegedly wronged plaintiffs can mean workers will be laid off, the value of the business may be seriously affected (affecting shareholders' equity), and the price of the business' products or services will increase to make up for the loss – if it doesn't first force them out of business. The medical community in North Carolina, Edwards' home state, has complained Edwards' firm alone had almost decimated it.*

...you admired Walter Mondale in his 1984 presidential run against Ronald Reagan for coming out against the F-14 fighter, the B-1 bomber and the M-1 tank (as well as a pay hike for the military), once again displaying liberals' tightfistedness with a buck when it comes to defending the country.

Ed. Note: *It seemed like déjà vu all over again with John Kerry running just 20 years later. Reagan's ultimate ratcheting-up of defense spending drove one of the final pegs in the Soviet coffin.*

⊰ ❋ ⊱

...you happily accepted Richard Clarke's charges (*Against All Enemies:* New York, Free Press, 2004) that, of the last four presidents only Bill Clinton performed effectively against terrorism, but was "weakened by continued political attack."

Ed. Note: *So far, it seems only Bill and Hillary seem to agree with Clarke, who resigned from the current administration as a disappointed office seeker. He thought he should have gotten Condi Rice's job, and his attitude shows in the book's somewhat dismissive treatment of her. Clarke also labeled Lynne Cheney, a "right-wing ideologue...like her husband."*

⊰ ❋ ⊱

...it seemed appropriate that Bill Clinton (along with Kofi Annan) should make it to Esquire magazine's 2nd Annual Best Dressed List. "They dress in a quietly elegant way which underlines their trustworthiness," said an Esquire representative. "This is true of Kofi Annan and it's true of Bill."

Ed. Note: *Do you think anyone at Esquire had the occasion to upchuck writing those lines about these two highly principled and moral stalwarts?*

⚹

...you agree that President Bush spends far too much time at the Western White House in Crawford, Texas, and should spend more days at the Washington White House, "takin' care of business."

Ed. Note: *That petty criticism is typical of liberals and ignores the fact that President Lyndon Johnson – a Democrat, remember – spent 450 days on vacation at his Texas ranch in his roughly five years in office, according to Ken Walsh, author of "From Mount Vernon to Crawford." That figures out to about 24 percent of his time in office.*

⚹

...you don't want to hear that Franklin Delano Roosevelt's administration during and after World War II was shot through with communist agents, including Lauchlin Currie (a former top aide); Harry Dexter White (head of the International Monetary Fund); and Alger Hiss, also a top aide and secretary-general at the founding of the United Nations.

Ed. Note: *In addition, Henry Wallace, who was FDR's vice president before Harry Truman, was a communist who founded the Progressive Party, which later was revealed to be controlled by Moscow.*

-¤ ✳ ¤-

...it was okay with you that President Jimmy Carter, while on vacations at the family retreat in Georgia, required military personnel carrying the missile codes needed in case of our nuclear response, to live off his property in Americus, 10 miles away.

Ed. Note: *Since a first strike could hit the continental U.S. in 15 to 20 minutes from launch, that's cutting it a little close.*

The Bill & Hill Show

"I think you can be an honest person and still lie about any number of things."

-- Dan Rather on President Bill Clinton

Should Hillary Rodham Clinton run in 2008 (a sure thing) and win (not so sure), America will have realized its first His & Hers presidencies. Should she win, I can't help but wonder what Madame President Clinton will have the carpenters do to that special White House office that Bill frequently used for...*defining the word "is."* Perhaps we can hold a contest for the best suggestions.

In any case, the inaugural major hurdle faced by the dysfunctional duo will be: *What do we call Bill*? You know: Last time around, Hillary was the *First Lady.* Now, some argue we should just retain that same designation for Bill.

There is a roundabout suggestion for that found in this piece of balanced and objective "news reporting" by *TIME* magazine's Margaret Carlson: "(Hillary) is the icon of American womanhood; she is the medium through which the remaining anxieties over feminism are being played out. Perhaps in addition to the other items on her agenda, Hillary Clinton will define for women that magical spot where the important work of the world and love and children and an inner life all come together. Like Ginger Rogers, she will do everything her partner does, only backward and in high heels…"

Beware when a professional journalist waxes effusive. Ms. Rodham Clinton might not have appreciated reading that she will do everything her partner does, "*only backward…*" Then again, since some already have accused her husband of doing things backward, Hillary then would be doing them… *forward. N'est ce pas*?

As for Margaret Carlson's reference to "high heels" – since the former president is a competitive kind of guy, even where his wife is concerned, it might be that Carlson was only speculating in her reportage suggesting a flat-footed Bill Clinton.

How about a compromise for right now, as long as we're not sure at this point who our 44th president will be? If Hillary does win it all, we can call Bill, the *First Laddie.*

Should Hillary win in 2008, we only can hope Bill doesn't interfere; and that as president, *she's her own man.* Or not? Hold that thought. In any case, in anticipation of a possible Clinton victory in '08, everyone should consider saving his shekels to defray the cost of an *overnight* in the Lincoln Bedroom.

...it slipped your memory that William Jefferson Clinton, back in 1992, promised the American people "the most ethical administration in the history of the Republic."

Ed. Note: *Of course, considering the word acrobatics for which the President would later become renowned, he never specified "<u>our</u> Republic." So cut him some slack, hey?*

...you "don't remember" that Bill Clinton made a 1992 campaign promise to cut taxes, only to turn around and actually raise them by a record $240 billion over a five-year period.

Ed. Note: *Clinton even allowed on one occasion in 1995, that people were still "mad at me" because he raised taxes too much. "Well, it might surprise you to know I think I raised them too much, too," he said with his boyish grin. However, that confession was not followed by a tax cut or rebate. Big surprise!*

...you agreed with then President Clinton when he pronounced: "Because it's not their money," as he attempted to explain why local school boards should not have more say in deciding how federal education dollars should be spent.

...to your way of thinking, during the 1992 presidential campaign, there was no reason to even hint at Bill Clinton's draft-dodging past, his participation in anti-war protests abroad, and his "sightseeing trip" to Moscow, a year after the Soviets crushed the Czechs' short-lived revolt.

Ed. Note:. *Of course, George H. W. Bush was labeled a "McCarthyite" and a "nut" for even broaching the subject.*

※

...you ignored Hillary Clinton's bone-chilling words that she "would trust big government over big business anytime."

Ed. Note: *Must be some special bottled water liberals drink. JFK once revealed that his dad had told him more than once, "all businessmen were sons of bitches." We never learned if old Joe included bootleggers among those SOBs.*

※

...it didn't bother you that President Clinton refused to crack down on terrorist-supporting Muslim charities, according to his senior advisor Dick Morris, "because of a fear that it would be seen as 'profiling' Islamic charities."

Ed. Note: *Yes, but Richard Clarke in his book said...*

※

...you didn't think it at all strange that R. James Woolsey, President Clinton's CIA director, revealed that through all of 1993 and 1994, he never had one private meeting with his boss.

Ed. Note: *What makes that all the more incredible is that it represents the timeframe for the first World Trade Center terrorist bombing. Yes, but Richard Clarke in his book said... By the way, "Monica Play the Harmonica" had plenty of private audiences with the Prez.*

❈

...if after an unbelievable amount of *smoke*, you still don't believe there were any *fires*, in various Clinton dealings, including Whitewater; the cattle futures incident (in which Hillary realized a 1000% return on her investment in 10 months); the Hasidic pardon of four New York residents on charges of defrauding the feds – after the area voted better than 10 to 1 to elect Sen. Hillary Clinton – and the acquittal of Bill Clinton's former finance director, also for fraud, after he threw a benefit to honor the President and raise funds for Hillary's 2000 senate campaign.

Ed. Note: *One guesses the old "walk like a duck, talk like a duck" adage doesn't apply to the Clintons.*

❈

...it was okay, even after Hillary emphatically denied she had done any legal work for the Castle Grande scam – which bilked taxpayers out of $3 million in the

1980s – that it later was proved she had drafted one of the bogus deal's central documents. That paperwork mysteriously disappeared during Bill's 1992 presidential campaign.

Ed. Note: *The woman who had been named one of the nation's top 100 lawyers by the National Law Journal finally was able to provide the documents in 1996, which inexplicably resurfaced in her White House bedroom. There never has been an explanation for that phenomenon.*

-ᵈ 💥 ᵇ-

...as far as you're concerned, Independent Counsel Ken Starr *obviously* was part of the "Vast Right-Wing Conspiracy" out to get President Clinton.

Ed. Note: *The puzzler is, if that were true about Starr, why did he rule that White House Deputy Counsel Vincent Foster, Jr., had committed suicide in 1993? Anyone out to get Clinton would have made as much political hay as possible out of such a "gift."*

-ᵈ 💥 ᵇ-

...you were satisfied with President Clinton's profoundly philosophical reply that it all "depends on what the meaning of the word '*is*' is," as he testified about his sexual imbroglio with White House intern Monica Lewinsky.

-ᵈ 💥 ᵇ-

...it meant nothing that the president made Monica Lewinsky a gift of Walt Whitman's *Leaves of Grass*, even though Ms. Lewinsky thought it was the "sort of gift that you wouldn't give someone that you didn't hold in a certain place in your heart."

Ed. Note: *Evidently, Hillary agreed with Monica, since Bill had given her the same gift many years before.*

❈

...you applauded President Clinton's decisive actions in bombing Iraq on December 19, 1998, because of Saddam Hussein's "nuclear, chemical and biological weapons program."

Ed. Note: *There was absolutely no correlation between the attack on Iraq and the beginning of Clinton's impeachment trial on the same day.. it says here.*

❈

...Bill Clinton was obviously correct that the "Vast Right-Wing Conspiracy," in true *Orwellian* fashion, was out to get him because it needed a new target after the Cold War ceased being a worthy one.

Ed. Note: *Just as Orwell wrote: One day we're fighting Eurasia, the next – Eastasia. Add a cup of paranoia to the old Clinton Family recipe, cookie.*

❈

...you missed the irony in Monica Lewinsky being a "little defensive" about a Grand juror calling her somewhat notorious garment a "cocktail dress," which certainly gave new definition to the term. Ms. Lewinsky preferred the term "work dress," which may be only slightly less risible.

Ed. Note: *Not greatly ballyhooed by the media at the time (big surprise!), official DNA testing revealed the odds in favor of the garment's stain being Bill Clinton's semen were 7.87 trillion to 1. Honest.*

—※—

…your favorite Clinton appointment was long, tall, pipe-smoking Attorney General Janet Reno, even though she actually was his third choice – because the first two women selected had illegal alien skeletons stashed away in their closets.

Ed. Note: *In the summer of 1995, Clinton confided to senior advisor Dick Morris that Reno was "his worst mistake." Many still believe it was Hillary all along who called the shots on appointing the Attorney General, which would explain why a man was never up for serious consideration for the post.*

—※—

…one of your favorite reads in 1996 was *It Takes a Village to Raise a Child*, by Hillary Rodham Clinton, which means you probably agreed with the author's assessment of public schools and how well equipped they are to provide a first-rate education to our kids.

Ed. Note: *Why didn't the Clintons send Chelsea to public school?*

-≡ ✵ ≡-

…you would have disagreed with some in the Clinton White House who wanted to use drivers' licenses to identify illegal aliens (during routine traffic violation stops) and deport them as a mean of combating terrorism.

Ed. Note: *"Profiling" was a major excuse for not doing it, which Clinton's people felt would have alienated the Hispanic vote, since they would have been caught up in the program as well. Better to put Americans of all races at risk, than take a chance pissing off Hispanic voters.*

-≡ ✵ ≡-

…you always enjoy the understated prose with which *TIME* magazine's Margaret Carlson (quoted earlier) manages to capture the essence of Hillary Clinton: "Secluded and quietly elegant [the new Clinton home], it has a spectacular garden in the back, with a pool tucked in amid hundred-year-old trees…Hilary wanted an instant Washington salon, as grand as her health care plan, with as many rooms as her ambition."

Ed. Note: *If Hillary does become the 44th President, don't be surprised if her White House director of communications turns out to be…Guess Who? By the way, "Guess Who" claims this brand of reporting is* *"down the middle." Question is, Ms. Carlson, what is it down the middle of?*

⊰ ❈ ⊱

...another *TIME* magazine piece on the brilliance that is Bill Clinton, also thrilled you by its description of Hillary as "the Woman Who Knew Too Much" and "sometimes can't help intimidating" voters with her knowledge.

Ed. Note: *Unfortunately, as much as she might have known, she wasn't talking —at least not about Whitewatergate, Travelgate, Cattlegate, Memogate and Lewinskygate. She might have had something to say about Billgates.*

⊰ ❈ ⊱

...it didn't bother you (though others might have turned green in the gills) when Dan Rather on CBS got into the act with this bit of objective reporting: "Once a political lightning rod, today she [Hillary] is political lightning. A crowd pleaser and first-class fund-raiser, a person under enormous pressure to step into the arena...polls show she is one of the most admired women in America,"

Ed. Note: *They didn't poll me or any of my friends. None of my enemies either.*

⊰ ❈ ⊱

...you hated NBC's Tim Russert for having the unconscionable gall to ask the First Lady a serious question about whether she would apologize for misleading Americans with her "vast right-wing conspiracy" statement, as well as her claim that the affair with Monica would not be "proven true."

Ed. Note: *Clinton neither apologized nor admitted misleading anybody. Tim Russert, on the other hand, was keelhauled by his media cohorts for playing the bully with the aggrieved First Lady.*

⚜

...you were not disturbed by Bill Clinton advisor George Stephanopoulos' revelations that anything emanating from the Clinton White House had better pass muster with Janet Reno's Justice Department; otherwise it wouldn't go anywhere because leaks would suddenly spring to compromise the activity, and the paperwork never would emerge from the bureaucracy – "unless the president typed it himself."

Ed. Note: *Question: Who the hell's in charge here?*

⚜

...you thought it kind of wistful and romantic that on the Clinton watch, perhaps more than 1,000 citizens were allowed to stay overnight in the White House Lincoln Bedroom – for a price, which ostensibly went to the Democratic National Committee.

Ed. Note: *Between sleepovers, seats on Air Force One, invitations to White House dinners, photo opps with the Clintons and/or Gores (depending on how many of* *them you could afford), and the right to eat in the White House kitchen, the Clinton Administration "sold" the American people's White House like never before or since. Chalk up a new low; and as a taxpayer and citizen...where's my cut?*

P.S. What would liberals have done to George Bush for similar activities? It's against the law to use the people's property (aka The White House) to raise funds for your political party

❈

...an unnatural alliance between President Clinton's administration and representatives of the People's Republic of China (PRC) did not bother you – though it meant appointing a PRC-affiliated individual to a sensitive U.S. post; waiving requirements for his Top Secret security clearance; providing him with highly classified briefings; and sharing sensitive technologies with the Chinese; all done for contributions to the Democratic National Committee.

Ed. Note: *Even the New York Times departed from its usual liberal kiss-up, America-bashing to comment, "Control of these sensitive technologies is too important to sacrifice for commercial gain, much less campaign contributions..." Guaranteed, had a Republican president done it, cries of "TREASON" would have reverberated in the halls of Congress, in elitist media news rooms and all across the blue states' landscape.*

❈

...you would have categorically believed Hillary Clinton, who labeled it "an outrageous lie," when she was accused of calling Paul Fray, who managed Bill Clinton's 1974 failed campaign for Congress, a "fucking Jew bastard."

Ed. Note: *At the time, Mary-Lee Fray, Paul's wife, and a Fray employee, both said, "It definitely happened."*

❈

...you doubted the veracity of Arkansas state trooper Larry Patterson, who told the media he had heard Hillary Clinton use similar anti-Semitic expletives on several occasions.

Ed. Note: *Trooper Patterson probably should have been decorated for valor, given the unfortunate events experienced in the careers of those who have blasphemed against Bill and Hill over the years.*

❈

...it did not bother you that video cable network VH1, a division of Viacom (which also owned CBS and Sen. Clinton's book publisher) actually edited out the audience *boos* and *heckling* which originally greeted Hillary's remarks to benefit 9/11 victims at a New York City concert.

Ed. Note: *Never one to miss turning a fast buck, VH1 released a DVD of the event in which only applause could be heard for the senator.*

❈

...you are not at all puzzled that Hillary and friends can't seem to get their stories straight about *what she knew and when, or even who told her* about Bill's trysts with Monica. She said the President told her, while Peter Baker, a Washington Post reporter, claimed Clinton attorney David Kendall was the one who gave her the news.

Ed. Note: *Sidney Blumenthal, one of the President's closest aides, said the couple was getting along well even right after Bill's grand jury appearance. That appears to contradict Hillary's statement that she could barely speak to him during that period.*

❈

...in the face of overwhelming opposition, you still backed Hillary Clinton's universal health care plan, which would, by all accounts, have put American health care essentially on the same level as that of Canada and England – countries whose patients in dire need, and physicians in dire disgust, both come to the U.S. for relief.

Ed. Note: *Another instance in which American grassroots common sense prevailed. Hoo, hah!*

What u̶n̶i̶t̶e̶d̶ Nations?

**"We must make sure that [the United Nations']
work is fruitful, that it is a reality and not sham,
that it is a force for action, and not merely a
frothing of words, that it is a true temple of peace
in which the shields of many nations can some day
be hung up, and not merely a cockpit in a Tower of
Babel."**

– Winston Churchill

From its very inception, and with few exceptions,
the United Nations has disappointed and fallen sadly
short of the ambitious role planned for it. In retrospect,
those aspirations probably were naïve.

A harbinger of things to come? Little known,
or conveniently forgotten is that not long after the
end of World War II, America introduced into the
fledgling United Nations something called the Baruch-
Lilienthal Plan. In the plan, the U.S. proposed turning
over its *nuclear monopoly* to an International Atomic
Development Authority "to which should be entrusted
all phases of the development and use of atomic
energy."

Most U.N. members enthusiastically applauded
the plan (that was before every kakistocracy of two
people or more, claiming to be a "nation," was eagerly
admitted to the General Assembly). Baruch-Lilienthal

meant there was a chance that nuclear power from that time on could be dedicated to peaceful purposes only.

Of course, the Soviet Union was able to kill the proposal with its veto (Churchill said, "*I told you so*"). Why did that happen? Because at that time, the USSR was too busy stealing "atomic" secrets from the U.S., Great Britain and elsewhere, prior to acquiring its own nuclear capability – for which it had definite plans.

In the 1940s, those liberals among us – *who had seen the future, and swore that it works* – were so smitten with "Uncle Joe," as FDR affectionately called Stalin, that they turned a blind eye to this obvious grab for a powerful new technology and the serious spoils of war it constituted for the Russian Bear; not to mention the fraught-filled future it held for everyone else.

The world's ensuing six decades could have been considerably more peaceful and positive had someone at the UN exhibited the *viscera* that had been so bravely spilled only a few years before on battlefields around the globe. But even then, the *Blame America First* liberals were able to excuse away the Soviet behavior because everybody knew the Russians were victims of a vicious policy known as "Western Encirclement." And so they further fed the Soviet paranoia.

From those days to these, things haven't changed all that much: *Hit the fast-forward button, Clyde:* It's May 2001, and the United States has been kicked off the UN Human Rights Commission, while *enlightened, virtuous paragons* such as Libya, Syria and Sudan are voted on as members. The action marked the first time the United States would not be represented on the Human Rights Commission since its creation in 1947.

The ineptitude and corruption of this kleptocracy known as the United Nations is sadly and dramatically underscored in Chapter 6 ("Impartial to Genocide") of former Israeli UN Ambassador Dore Gold's *Tower of Babble* (New York: Crown Forum, 2004). It documents the insane and shameful malfeasance of the UN in failing to protect an estimated 800,000 Rwandans – mostly Tutsi tribesmen – from being massacred by the Hutus, their fellow Rwandans, in the mid-1990s. Before we go on, think of that: Upwards of 800,000 human beings slaughtered – <u>more than four times the population of the city in which the author lives</u>. Most of the massacre was permitted because the UN did not wish to appear to be taking sides in the matter.

We could go into the "Oil for Food" and sundry other scandals – still brewing as this goes to press – but the evidence has been pretty well exposed, and it's clear that someone, or more appropriately, many *someones*, have nailed another peg into the UN coffin. If ever there were a compelling argument for something needing to be stripped down and put back together from scratch – and very differently – it applies most definitely to the United Nations. It may already be too late for this Humpty-Dumpty.

One virtually could eliminate from membership half those countries now in the General Assembly and relatively few people would notice. They act only as a negative energy source within the UN, and shamefully misrepresent the interests of their countrymen. The only people benefiting from their temporary relocation in Manhattan are the countries' representatives themselves. It's time to cut bait. They've enjoyed paved roads, clean drinking water and indoor plumbing long enough.

In fact, the time is long past due that the UN's host country should "buy back its invitation," and encourage that august body to relocate its headquarters to a new venue – perhaps a country more hungry for the prestige. France comes to mind.

Besides, New Yorkers would love to reclaim all those illegal parking spots now being usurped by official limos sporting diplomatic flags; and think of the increased revenues for the city coffers once all those late parking ticket fees start rolling in.

...you fervently believe that today's United Nations is the dynamic world body that can move quickly, decisively and resolutely to maintain world peace and otherwise protect those potential victims of state-sponsored genocide.

❈

...you watched with mild interest while UN diplomats haggled in New York over the Rwandan issue, a period that embraced a 100-day killing spree in the spring-summer of 1994 – which culminated in the massacre of 800,000 African tribesmen by the Hutu tribe.

Ed. Note: *In one of those, "it's too horrible to be ironic" footnotes, the representative of Rwanda's Hutu-dominated government was sitting on the UN Security Council for that entire period, repeatedly denying that any genocide was under way.*

❈

...you may simply have missed the fact that the UN ordered a Belgian peacekeeping force to withdraw its protection from a technical school in Rwanda, where it had been protecting 2,000 refugees, including 400 children, from the Hutu militia – which was cooling its heels outside drinking beer. With the Belgian withdrawal complete, the Hutu went in firing machine guns and throwing grenades. Most of the refugees were killed immediately.

Ed. Note: *The Belgian "peacekeeping" troops were operating under the auspices of (ready for this?) **UNAMIR**, which stands for United Nations Assistance Mission for **R**wanda... Please, no more "assistance."*

◄ ❋ ►

...despite the fact that Saddam Hussein had ignored or violated 16 Security Council resolutions over a 12-year period, you still believe the U.S. should have *waited* for the UN to do something significant about Iraq.

Ed. Note: *After all, Hussein did show good faith by kicking out UN inspectors.*

◄ ❋ ►

...you advocate a status quo situation between the United States and the world's largest international debating society, which effectively means that an assertive personality such as John Bolton has no place in the office of U.S. Ambassador to the UN.

Ed. Note: *The current functioning of the UN is exactly the way liberals like their government – a bloated bureaucracy bogged down in stultifying debate, which means no action and therefore no risks need be taken.*

◄ ❋ ►

...you were shocked that President Bush would appoint John "Damaged Goods" Bolton to serve as U.S. ambassador to the U.N., especially right after congress – including the small, vocal minority who disapproved

– recessed in August and was unable to do anything about it.

Ed. Note: *Liberals' latest Bolton mantra, "damaged goods," failed to note that it was the liberals who attempted to damage those goods. If a shopper in a store breaks an item, he is expected to pay for those "damaged goods."*

❈

...it doesn't bother you that the UN in 2002 created an International Criminal Court (ICC), which, if convened against Americans could deny us the right to a trial by a jury of our peers, and otherwise suspend our rights of constitutionally protected guarantees to a fair trial and due process. To agree to the legitimacy of such a court would, for the first time, acknowledge the authority of an institution not elected by the American people, nor accountable to them, but one that could prosecute them.

Ed. Note: *As called for by some members of the liberal media, the ICC could be used to try the president and U.S. troops for "war crimes."*

❈

...you found it acceptable that in 2003, a coalition of "legal experts and human rights organizations" announced it would go to the ICC to prosecute the U.S. for alleged war crimes during the most recent war with Iraq. But because the U.S. was not a signatory to the

ICC, the group decided to go after Great Britain, which had signed, and is America's staunchest ally.

Ed. Note: *Ironically, on that same day, the UN nominated to the Human Rights Commission the countries of Cuba; the Democratic Republic of Congo; Egypt; Iran; Nigeria; North Korea; Russia and Saudi Arabia – every one of them a paragon of human rights.*

⊰ ✻ ⊱

...you don't mind that the United Nations also has designs on American kids as well. A UNESCO (United Nations Educational, Scientific and Cultural Organization) brochure on educational goals for students states, "As long as the child breathes the poisoned air of nationalism, education in world-mindedness can produce only rather precarious results."

Ed. Note: *"World-mindedness" is one of those buzz terms that's also used to justify the redistribution of wealth among the have-nots, can-nots and will-nots. More recently, the UN has expressed interest in assuming "international control" over the Internet, which is a U.S. invention. Just ask Al Gore.*

⊰ ✻ ⊱

...it makes perfectly good sense to you that Syria, although listed by the U.S. as a country long supporting terrorism (including in the aftermath of the Iraq war) should have been awarded a seat on the UN Security

Council; and in fact has even chaired the Security Council more than once since 2001.

Ed. Note: *Syria secured 160 "yes" votes of the 177 nations voting on the first ballot.*

⊶ ✳ ⊷

...you don't see any problem with Syria having taken possession of Lebanon for 20 years and yet being invited by the UN to join its Security Council.

Ed. Note: *That morality reversal turned Lebanon into a host for more than a dozen pro-Syrian terrorist organizations.*

⊶ ✳ ⊷

...you've apparently forgotten that John Kerry, who advocated a "global test" for U.S. foreign policy (read: acting only with approval of the UN) during the last presidential election, did not win that election.

⊶ ✳ ⊷

...it apparently hasn't sunk in that as long as the United States keeps sending the same kind of individual to the UN to serve as our ambassador, we are going to continue to reap the same results, which cannot appeal to any Americans unless they possess the "Blame America First" mentality.

⊶ ✳ ⊷

...you saw nothing wrong with the rude and hostile behavior of Democrats on the Foreign Relations

Committee questioning presumptive UN Ambassador John Bolton – specifically Senators Barbara Boxer (Calif.) and Russ Feingold (Wisc.), both of whom treated Bolton as though he were a foreign national opposed to American policies, instead of an American chosen for the post by the president.

Ed. Note: *Boxer accused Bolton of "having nothing but disdain for the United Nations;" Feingold told Bolton, "You appear to believe the UN. is at best irrelevant and at most harmful." So what's their point?*

❈

…fervently you still believe that pulling coalition troops out of the Middle East and giving the United Nations a chance to "work its magic" on militant Muslims will help ensure Americans their future safety.

❈

…you were impressed – as one infatuated with bloated bureaucracy – that the United Nations multiplied seven-fold its worldwide peacekeepers between 1988 and 1994 (11,000 to 78,000), mainly made possible by the dissolution of the Soviet Union.

Ed. Note: *But true to form, it was the proverbial tale told by an idiot, full of sound and fury, signifying nothing – as the UN allowed the competing interests of member states to once again render it impotent.*

❈

...the fact that Iraq was named head of the UN Disarmament Conference in January 2003, even with heated diplomatic negotiations and frantic weapons inspections going on at the time, didn't strike you as being particularly asinine.

-= ❋ =-

...you were indignant over Ronald Reagan's response to the United Nations condemning the U.S. invasion of Grenada. Said the president, "It didn't upset my breakfast at all."

-= ❋ =-

...the idea of UN impotence in world affairs was not brought home to you by the fact that the president of the Security Council issued a minimum of 30 statements acknowledging Saddam Hussein's repeated violations of U.N. resolutions; none of which accomplished anything positive.

-= ❋ =-

...it still wasn't enough proof for you of United Nations malfeasance when a UN detachment of troops responsible for guarding Rwandan Chief Justice Joseph Kovaruganda, instead turned him over to a Hutu death squad, then stood laughing and drinking with his killers as they assaulted the judge's wife and daughters.
Ed. Note: *The UN confirmed the details in its official inquiry.*

...in order to reinforce your argument that President Bush concocted the idea of Weapons of Mass Destruction (WMD) to justify war against Iraq, you ignored remarks by David Kay, head of the CIA Iraq Survey Group. Kay said that the interrogations of former Iraqi officials revealed that "a lot of material" went to Syria before the war, including "some components of Saddam's WMD program."

Ed. Note: *The United Nations Monitoring, Verification, and Inspection Commission (UNMOVIC) agreed with that assessment in June 2004.*

※

...the admission by UN Secretary General Kofi Annan that the UN had "an institutional ideology of impartiality even when confronted with attempted genocide," did not send a chill down your spine.

Ed. Note: *Perhaps one should first check that there is a spine in place down which a chill might be sent.*

※

...it troubled you not that Kofi Annan's Department of Peacekeeping Operations instructed a UN general in Rwanda: "You should make every effort not to compromise your impartiality or to act beyond your mandate." In which case, countless thousands of Africans were slaughtered while the U.N. focused on "impartiality."

Ed. Note: *What's really needed is a new definition of "impartiality."*

...you did not laugh up your sleeve when Boutros Boutros-Ghali, UN secretary-general at the time of the Rwanda massacre, pleaded ignorance to many of the horrific events going on in Africa, claiming he was "away from the UN headquarters… throughout most of January 1994."

Ed. Note: *What makes it even more risible is that Boutros-Ghali's handpicked personal representative (who could not plead ignorance) was named Jacques-Roger Booh-Booh. In short, you might say the UN secretary-general committed a big booh-booh*

...you did not see any point in hurrying things after Saddam Hussein was given 15 days by the UN (Resolution #687) to declare his stashes of prohibited WMD in the aftermath of the 1991 Gulf War. Twelve years later Hussein still had not made a complete disclosure.

Ed. Note: *Perhaps the Butcher of Baghdad, like Boutros-Ghali, also was out of town at the time – "throughout most of 12 years."*

...you thought the Rwanda disgrace was a UN aberration until it was repeated only one year later in Bosnia, when the Serbs attacked Muslims in a UN "safe area," slaughtering an estimated 7,000 in Srebrenica and deporting 40,000 more to other parts of Bosnia.

Ed. Note: *Dutch troops defending under the UN flag simply abandoned Srebrenica. But not before their commander repeatedly called for massive air strikes, which the commander of all UN forces in the region (a French general) refused.*

※

...if it didn't strike you as strange that the UN refused to properly insert itself into Rwanda or Bosnia to prevent those massacres. But a 2002 Israeli-Palestinian battle, for which the Palestinians claimed Israeli atrocities, did draw a UN fact-finding team and a resolution – which focused its investigation not on the Palestinian attack, but on the Israeli defenders responding to the attack.

※

...you found it neither laughable nor despicable that just one month after 9/11, the Nobel Peace Prize would be awarded to Kofi Annan and the United Nations.

Ed. Note: *And, not content with that gaucherie, one year later Nobel would similarly favor Jimmy Carter for his opposition to his country's war on terror.*

※

...it didn't alarm you that even Iran displayed contempt for the United Nations, when it shrugged off the threat that the International Atomic Energy Agency may refer it to the UN Security Council if it resumes uranium processing.

Ed. Note: *Underscoring its lack of respect for the UN's ability to act decisively and effectively, Iran's foreign minister said, "We are not concerned and are ready for anything."*

⊰ ❊ ⊱

...you believe the UN can get along without the U.S., but don't think the U.S. can act viably without the UN.

Ed. Note: *Can't we at least test the theorem to see who's right?*

A Final Word...or Two

This book did not start out as a *book*. Originally it was to be a personal journal, a compendious reminder of liberal duplicity – a *living* document for my own handy reference – in which particularly illuminating entries from readings and other sources could be conveniently catalogued for easy referral. It was only after the decision was made to "book it," that I started adding the "**Ed. Note.**" feature at the end of many of the items. Prior to that, I only reserved those nasty thoughts for myself.

Before the reader gets the wrong idea, I'm not a compulsive personality, nor am I paranoid (but *they* are out to get us, aren't they?). I just needed to have a personal collection of such ideas on paper because I have any number of liberal friends with whom I'm at loggerheads over various issues from time to time. So I wanted to have this stuff documented.

While the title of the book is admittedly a *knock-off* of Jeff Foxworthy's very funny series, even that was not intentionally orchestrated – *I'm not sure how it came about.* All I know is, one Saturday morning in early July, I suddenly awoke at 2:15 on the sofa in the den where I'd fallen asleep while watching television. The TV was droning on with some infomercial at the time.

Curiously, I realized the words, *"You may be a liberal if...,"* were unmistakably bouncing around inside my skull. I didn't know why. I'd never read one of Foxworthy's books, nor seen his TV show. I did vaguely recall having seen him in a TV guest appearance some years before, and I knew I had read something about him some time in the past. So I couldn't claim ignorance of Foxworthy or his work. I have since bought one of his books in a hopeful search for clues to that early morning epiphany in July. But I haven't found any answers.

The disparate worlds of country culture and liberal politics are mutually exclusive as far as I know.

In any case, I immediately wrote the title down on a paper pad, one of a number I keep around the house because I have the memory retention of a gnat, especially at 2:15 in the morning. Then I went back to sleep. A few hours later when I was awake and on my second cup of coffee, I started on *the book*. Twenty-four hours earlier had you asked about *the book*, my quizzical reply would have been, "What book?"

I put it together because I'm sure – *I hope* – there are many others like me who are disturbed (should I rephrase that?) and at least a little concerned for America's future. So I thought if I could compress this stuff into a relative few pages – a sampling of what I saw as a kind of treachery existing today in our country – and make that sampling easily accessible to others, then maybe I will have done someone a good turn; something I admit I'm not accustomed to doing.

I've never been one to see an insidious scheme or a nefarious plot under every rock or behind every tree, and I don't believe that's the case today. But I do detect an elitist smarminess among many of our leaders or leader-*wannabes*, who seem to be more interested in advocating what's trendy or contrary (often the same thing), to the exclusion of everyday *common sense*.

That may be acceptable when we're dealing in the world of high fashion or the art cosmos. After all, some people still swear by Andy Warhol's soup cans, or fawn over godawful fashions that make women look like truck drivers in drag. But it's not acceptable when you're shooting craps with a world my grandkids (and yours) will inherit, especially since the little guys have no say in the matter right now. It's our stewardship.

I don't find it fashionable to disparage the flag... or to demand my neighbors tear down their nativity scene...or to forego teaching the basics in school in favor of "social engineering"...or to screw up the syntax of a nicely crafted sentence just because it may not be politically correct. I was never a public relations *spokesperson*. I was a public relations *spokesman*.

As long as it doesn't hurt me and mine, leave it alone. Why the need to insinuate yourself into another's life if he didn't invite you? Now to me, that's *sophistication*. The intelligence and forbearance to allow people to do what gives them pleasure, or instills pride and makes them feel good about themselves – as long as it's not intrinsically harmful to others. It's called self-determination and responsibility.

Supreme Court Justice John Marshall Harlan recognized that freedom contains within itself the possibility that we may not always make the wisest decisions, that we may at times act "irresponsibly" – but that no person is truly free who is not permitted occasionally to be...*irresponsible.*

Even liberal *New York Times* columnist Tom Wicker has written, "The highest freedom of all may well be the freedom to conduct one's life and affairs responsibly – but by one's own standards of responsibility."

Did you ever notice that those out there who are least capable of telling the rest of us how to live our lives, are usually the ones most willing and anxious to do just that?

Franklyn S. Haiman, formerly professor of communications at Northwestern U., noted in his *Speech and Law in a Free Society,* that even if we were not the best judges of our own interests, "it is infinitely more dangerous to try and determine *who is* best equipped to make decisions for themselves."

For more than two-and-a-quarter centuries Americans (in the most simplistic terms) have been doing things in certain ways that have brought us to the present day as world leader. It was not a mantle most of us set out to assume because, after all, a good part of it was not orchestrated – it was accidental.

Those were years marked by absolutely sublime accomplishment and tragic human failing. In all, we are today the sum total of those miracles and those miscues. Chapter after chapter of America's history has chronicled our triumphs and limned our disasters. But in all that long history, it seemed the one constant Americans could fall back on was an innate *common sense*; "horse sense," some of our forebears called it.

Unfortunately, some of us have lost that horse sense somehow, somewhere along the way. For purposes of this document, let's call those people...oh, I dunno... *liberals*. I recognize two distinct groups among liberals – one a little dumb, one a *lot* treacherous.

The first group consists of younger, perhaps naïve individuals, who are genuinely idealistic and not yet tempered by life's experiences to have arrived at a more common sense approach to the issues and how to deal with them. They spend so much of the day with their heads in the clouds searching for rainbows, that they usually wind up stepping in dog shit a goodly portion of the time. Often they vote the way they vote because that's how mom and pop before them voted. I used to joke about my dad (not to his face, of course), that if the Democrats ran a chimpanzee for office (whether in Chicago or D.C.), he'd be in the voting booth pulling the lever for J. Fred Muggs every time.

The offspring of these veteran voters are usually the ones who mouth all the tiresome platitudes about America going to war in order to grab the other guy's oil…that every tax cut is aimed mainly at the rich…and that non-liberal domestic programs will end up starving poor children and their welfare-dependent mothers. Pardon me, I guess we call them "entitlements" today, don't we? The point is, they follow the *ideologues,* including their college professors, because it's so much easier and more convenient than having to think for themselves.

Then, there's the second group: These guys are also dumb, but in different ways. They're dumb despite the fact they should know better. These are the cynics, the jaded, oftentimes ruthless individuals who are not naïve, but also are not above playing the *disingenuous* card in order to accomplish their ends – without any regard for the means that got them there. These are the guys who latch on to those in the first group and exploit their trust and their energies, and sometimes-blind allegiances to noble sounding ideologies. They lie with straight faces, but feign indignation when they're caught at it.

Of these two *dumb* groupings, I can tolerate the former over the latter.

I refuse to believe that during this time of war, many liberal leaders don't know exactly the harm they're doing to America's security – with their constant and mean-spirited, back-biting duplicity and petty fault-finding. They'll use any tools at their disposal – anything – to discredit the opposition in order to make it easier for themselves, always with an avaricious eye cocked toward the next election. That's what liberals do.

Everybody wants to win. But is winning worth putting your country at risk by trying to dismantle its efforts to protect citizens against a fanatical enemy? Often a win at any cost turns out to be a pyrrhic victory. And it's just not enough to decide an administration policy is *wrong* – you have to advance something better.

Of course, you can't blame the Democrats entirely. In one of those "blue moon" situations where one party controls the Presidency *and* the Congress, the Republicans act as if it's an embarrassment of riches for them. They have a golden opportunity to set things straight for their country for some time to come, but they seem hell-bent intent on frittering it away. You've got to hand it to the Democrats. If the situation were reversed, the GOP would have been screaming "uncle" long before now. You just know that.

Liberals like to claim they're the "loyal opposition" and have the right, nay, the *duty* to oppose. And they are absolutely correct. That's one of the linchpins of a healthy democracy. But once again, they *know* the difference between honest discourse required to address a real problem in order to advance this nation's interests – as opposed to their own, self-serving, grasping-at-straws to fabricate or blow out of proportion some oftentimes phantom issue, mostly for the purpose of scoring points against the administration.

This is a time of war and we simply can't afford the same brand of partisan nonsense we've come to expect from Capitol Hill in peacetime – not now while madmen are trying to kill our troops in the Middle East and the rest of us elsewhere.

Here are some random talking points to ponder about liberals that helped influence me to put this screed together – personal *blood boilers* for me. I'm sure you have your own:

- Doesn't shame play any role in our lives anymore? How can a former president of the United States, impeached and disbarred from practicing the law (though not one Democrat in the Senate voted to turn him out), continue to strut the world stage as though it never happened? Doesn't it bother him that he single-handedly dragged the American presidency down to new lows of morality? For argument's sake, substitute in that scenario a <u>Republican</u> president who was getting *his hanky pankied* while in office. Would liberals ever, ever, ever, have let up with the fusillades of opprobrium and acrimony? *Yes, that is a rhetorical question.*

- Bill Clinton should thank his Maker that Jimmy Carter preceded him as president. It saved Clinton from being perceived as the most inept chief executive of the 20th century. He still holds title for *most morally bankrupt*, however. The Guinness Book probably doesn't have to worry about that one being challenged anytime soon.

- Clinton continues to enjoy praise and accolades showered on him. While a re-elected U.S. president, in the middle of a war with fanatics dedicated to killing us, is constantly lambasted for everything from a "failed" search for WMDs to an alleged, less-than-beaming intellect…from his motivations for attacking Iraq to his employ of an election campaign architect (whom the Democrats would dearly love to hire)…from failed British intelligence to the leftist-exploited grief of a dead soldier's mother.

- Nobody has suggested that if Clinton had met with his CIA director *privately* – only half as many times as he had with a libidinous White House intern – he might have helped derail future terrorist attacks. The fact is, he never met with James Woolsey privately all through 1993 and 1994, the timeframe for the original WTC terrorist attack. Like Alice in Wonderland, everything is topsy-turvy.

- Does Teddy Kennedy really believe the Iraq War was planned in Crawford, Texas, months prior to WTC, as he's stated with unflinching, absolute conviction? Where's the proof? How irresponsible is that? But Kennedy is famous (infamous?) for spitting out inflammable

175

rhetoric without offering a scintilla of proof, and then expecting everybody to swallow it because...*he's Kennedy*. And, because they've been swallowing it in Massachusetts for the last 110 years during which he's held office – even before the incident at *Cop-a-quick-one*, or whatever they called that river.

- How can a CBS anchorman finally recognize that a bogus report on a sitting president's military record is exactly that – *bogus*; but then turn around and in the very next breath insist that the story is legitimate just the same? How can a national newsman at a national network make such claims without proof? *Everybody* at CBS News should have been consigned to the ash heap for that one.

- How is it possible America can be so wrong so much of the time...as far as liberals are concerned? Less so, of course, when Democrats are in control.

- The liberal mantra seems to be: *"I oppose this, that and the other things the American hoi polloi recognize [including the deity, flag, family, memorials, the police, the military – seemingly any traditions that glue Americans together]. That opposition shows I am cosmopolitan, a sophisticated internationalist, who is not swayed by the bourgeois arguments of patriotism. I do not ascribe such good intentions to Americans as you would have me believe exist. Perhaps I will allow that many of the Great Uunwashed are well meaning, but so many of their leaders – those of a conservative bent – are big businesss-oriented, unsympathetic to the poor and simplistically patriotic. The people on the other hand, are little more than sheep, blindly believing and bleating after the arrogant, fairy-tale assumption that America is the greatest nation on earth. Such an attitude is anathema to the concept of one-worldliness, which can be accomplished only if the U.S. subordinates itself to the World Body in the name of all humankind."* Or something like that.

- Liberals can be extremely mean and cruel in their denunciations of people, who in some way may thwart them; mean and cruel in a terribly spiteful and petty way – only as one mean *little girl* can be cruel to another – somehow able to come up with just the perfectly nasty thing to say that penetrates like an insidiously sharp paper cut. When veteran CBS reporter Bernard Goldberg left the network and wrote his bestseller, *Bias,* Tom Shales (the *Washington Post* TV reporter, of all things) called the *Emmy Award* winner "a no-talent hack," and a "full-time addlepated windbag," among many other choice expletives.

- Linda Tripp, erstwhile buddy to Monica Lewinsky, was labeled by the liberal media as "ugly and evil" and the "hulking dikey one;" mainly of course because it was Tripp's involvement that implicated Bill Clinton. Interestingly, more criticism was leveled at Tripp by the mainstream media than at Clinton and Lewinsky put together. Liberals admire whistle blowers, as long as it's the liberals on the business end of the whistle. *Ask not for whom the whistle blows, it blows for thee.*

- And it's not just a recent practice. You can go back to Whittaker Chambers, who ratted out the communist spy Alger Hiss in 1948, and you'll learn that Chambers was "dirty and ill-kempt." He always appeared disheveled, as though he "had spent the night on a park bench," and with "bad teeth" (the press liked to harp on that one). Let's see, what else? Oh, yes, Chambers also was a homosexual, who'd had an affair with his own brother, Richard; whom Alger Hiss' attorney insisted on calling "Dickie." Those last charges, by the way, were atrocious lies, and the liberals knew it.

- But you *never* see or hear conservatives treating liberals in that fashion. Not that conservatives *don't think it*, mind you. For example, I *could think* that the liberal half of a popular TV news team physically reminds me of nothing less than a bomb-throwing Bolshevik – with that *faux* European haircut, geeky pencil neck and the smarmy little smile. Keep the glasses and put a Greek fisherman's cap on him, and he looks just like one of those Communist toadies you'd see running around Red Square in every Russian Revolution movie ever made. Now that's what I might say if I were to borrow a page from liberals. Fortunately, I'm above that sort of thing.

- I have problems fathoming the mentality that fabricates such egregious put-downs. Coming from otherwise well educated, presumably well-bred professionals, why does that happen? Can you really hate someone with such a white-hot intensity?

- Closely related to the above, liberals also have had a tendency, when they dispute someone over an issue, to quickly attack their opponent if they feel they're losing the debate. It's called an *ad hominem* argument. The tactic is, if you make your opponent look bad, you discredit his argument as well. It actually can work if the audience is unfamiliar with the practice – or they happen to be on the liberal's side to begin with.

- Another thing: Liberals have no discernible sense of humor. When President Reagan joked about the Soviets into a radio microphone that he didn't realize was live, he sent legions of liberals scurrying for their Tums and Maalox.

This catharsis could go on ad nauseam, and probably has for some readers. I beg your indulgence. But before I put it out of its misery, I'd like to suggest to anybody out there who may be interested in how truly to appreciate the nonsensical world we live in (because only then can we begin to fix it), that they pick up a copy of *The Death of Common Sense: How the Law is Suffocating America* by Philip K. Howard (New York: Warner Books, 1994).

It's a great jumping-off point, and it will hold your interest while making an attractive argument for something that should concern *social environmentalists* – the impending demise of common sense. *It* is an endangered species. But don't allow your liberal friends(?) to read it. They probably will glue the pages together out of spite – even though that means the wasteful death of another tree.

Part of the liberal problem is that they've pretty much had it their own way for too long, certainly as far as the media go – which is saying a lot in our news hungry culture. It used to be difficult for an objective story to find its way out of the liberal media maze without getting spun; and as for the emergence of a positive story with right-of-center implications to it – forget it! That wasn't going to happen.

But all that is changing, rapidly and of necessity, and it had better. The pendulum swings, the sands shift and we inhabit a world in which this country's best interests are not served by a liberal philosophy – if ever they were. Liberalism does not work in a world in which America must move forthrightly and react quickly as a possible condition of our survival – a world in fact, in which there is precious little "wiggle-room" for reaction because the daily realities require that we be proactive and positive.

America cannot hand over its future to a "world order," which continues to demand more *of everything* from us on the one hand, while attempting to subjugate us to its *universality* and *sovereignty* on the other. That's why American liberalism continues its downward spiral toward irrelevancy and, even more importantly, why the rest of us cannot follow down that dark and dank tunnel. To do so abrogates the futures of our children and their children's children.

With the advent and whopping success of the Fox News Channel; with popular conservative radio talk show hosts like Rush Limbaugh, Bill O'Reilly, Michael Reagan, Sean Hannity and Michael Savage; with Brent Bozell's Media Research Center, which "watchdogs" the liberal press; and with the ascendancy of publishing houses willing to take on conservative writers–publishers such as Regnery Publishing, Crown Forum, Rutledge Hill Press and Nelson Current – liberals today often find themselves playing an unfamiliar role – on the defensive side of the ball.

And that's a good thing!

Acknowledgments

The following sources, listed alphabetically, provided information and inspiration for *You May Be A Liberal If....*

A National Party No More, The Conscience Of A Conservative Democrat, Zell Miller (Atlanta, Ga.: Stroud & Hall, 2003)

Against All Enemies, Inside America's War on Terror, Richard A. Clarke (New York: Free Press, 2004)

An Underground Education, The Unauthorized And Outrageous Supplement To Everything You Thought You knew About Art, Sex, Business, Crime, Science, Medicine, And Other Fields Of Human Knowledge, Richard Zacks (New York: Doubleday, 1997)

Arrogance, Rescuing American from the Media Elite, Bernard Goldberg (New York: Warner Books, 2003)

Bias, A CBS Insider Exposes How the Media Distort the News, Bernard Goldberg (New York: Perennial, 2003)

Big Fat Liars, How Politicians, Corporations, And The Media Use Science And Statistics To Manipulate The Public, Morris E. Chafetz, M.D. (Nashville, Tenn.: Nelson Current, 2005)

Deliver Us From Evil, Sean Hannity (New York: ReganBooks, 2004)

Don't Know Much About History, Everything You Need to Know About American History but Never Learned, Kenneth C. Davis (New York: Avon Books, 1990)

High Crimes and Misdemeanors, The Case Against Bill Clinton, Ann Coulter (Washington, D.C.: Regnery Publishing, Inc., 1998)

How To Talk To A Liberal (If You Must), The World According to Ann Coulter, Ann Coulter (New York: Crown Forum, 2004)

Intellectual Morons, How Ideology Makes Smart People Fall For Stupid Ideas, Daniel J. Flynn (New York: Crown Forum, 2004)

Liberalism Is A Mental Disorder, Michael Savage (Nashville, Tenn.: Nelson Current, 2005)

Lies (And the Lying Liars Who Tell Them), A Fair and Balanced Look at the Right, Al Franken (New York: Dutton, 2003)

Lies My Teacher Told Me, James W. Loewen (New York: The New Press, 1995)

Media Resource Center, *"America's Media Watchdog,"* Washington. D.C.

Off With Their Heads, Traitors, Crooks & Obstructionists In American Politics, Media & Business, Dick Morris (New York: ReganBooks, 2003)

Slander, Liberal Lies About the American Right, Ann Coulter (New York: Three Rivers Press, 2002)

The Enemy Within, Michael Savage (Nashville, Tenn.: WND Books, 2003)

The Fall Of The Berlin Wall, William F. Buckley Jr. (Hoboken, N.J.: John Wiley & Sons, Inc., 2004)

The Official Handbook Of The Vast Right-Wing Conspiracy, The Arguments You Need To Defeat The Loony Left, Mark W. Smith (Washington, D.C., Regnery Publishing, Inc., 2004)

The Politically Incorrect Guide to American History, Thomas E. Woods, Jr., Ph.D. (Washington, D.C.: Regnery Publishing, Inc., 2004)

Tower Of Babble, How The United Nations Has Fueled Global Chaos, Dore Gold (New York: Crown Forum, 2004)

Treason, Liberal Treachery From The Cold War To The War On Terrorism, Ann Coulter (New York: Crown Forum, 2003)

Useful Idiots, How Liberals Got It Wrong in the Cold War and Still Blame America First, Mona Charen (Washington, D.C.: Regnery Publishing, Inc., 2004)

Venona, Decoding Soviet Espionage in America, John Earl Haynes & Harvey Klehr (New Haven, Conn.: Yale Nota Bene, 2000)

Weapons Of Mass Distortion, The Coming Meltdown of the Liberal Media, L. Brent Bozell III (New York: Crown Forum, 2004)

Why Do People Hate America?, Ziauddin Sardar & Merryl Wyn Davies (New York: The Disinformation Company, Ltd., 2002)

You Might Be A Redneck If...This Is The Biggest Book You've Ever Read, Jeff Foxworthy (Nashville, Tenn.: Rutledge Hill Press, 2004)

About The Author

Bob Sagan is a Nevada-based communications consultant in marketing, advertising, media and public relations. An award-winning writer, he also has worked as a journalist and continues to freelance for newspapers and magazines across the country. His columns and articles have appeared in more than 300 publications nationally and abroad.

Sagan is scheduled for an extended trip to Africa in late 2005. From Kenya he will report for some 40 North American media outlets on a joint U.S.-Canadian humanitarian project to build recreational facilities for Kenyan children, including orphans who have lost their parents to an AIDS epidemic in this "top tier of all AIDS/HIV countries." He is planning a book on the experience.

He is not a liberal.